Eyewitness to Promise:

Abraham

Eyewitness to Promise:

Abraham

Mindy Ferguson

AMG Publishers, Inc. | amgpublishers.com

Eyewitness Bible Studies
Eyewitness to Promise: Abraham
Copyright © 2018 by Mindy Ferguson

Published by AMG Bible Studies, an imprint of AMG Publishers, Chattanooga, Tennessee (www.amgpublishers.com).

ISBN XX: 978-0-89957-911-5

First AMG Printing—January 2018

Cover art direction by Brian Woodlief, Chattanooga, TN.
Interior design by PerfecType, Nashville, TN.
Typesetting, editing and proofreading by Nord Compo, Lille, France

Printed in USA

18 19 20 POD 3 2 1

DEDICATION

This study is dedicated with love to

The Ferguson Family in Texas, Florida, Colorado, Utah, Illinois, and Georgia.

Your steady relationships with God through the ups and downs of life,
your commitment to do the right thing, even when it is painful,
and your dedication to family have inspired me greatly—
in life and in ministry.

CONTENTS

Week 4: Matters of Preservation

Week 5: Opposing Offspring

Week 6: Refining Revelations

Week 7: Significant Conclusions

Week 8: Blessed to Bless

INTRODUCTION

When God told Abraham to leave his country, his people, and his father's household (Genesis 12:1), Abraham obeyed, even though he had no idea where he was going (Hebrews 11:6). Despite cultural and family pressures, Abraham persevered along his journey of faith and eventually became the father of a nation, just as God promised.

The cultural pressures of our modern-day society are powerful and more influential than at any time in my memory. Living according to godly principles is rare. Standing firm on the truths of God's Word is risky. Navigating life God's way is ridiculed. But God is faithful, and His promises are true.

Through this study, you will travel with Abraham along his faith journey. As you watch this budding father of nation question God's plans, take matters into his own hands, and, at times, compromise truth, you will recognize God's faithfulness with every misstep. If you are like me, you will relate to Abraham's mistakes and be encouraged by his growth. As you journey with this great man of faith through the pages of God's Word, like Abraham, I trust you will develop a more unwavering faith that will inspire you to become a greater blessing to others. You, too, will become an eyewitness to the promise of our God.

About This Study

The book of Genesis includes the account of Abraham as he and his wife, Sarah, traveled with God to the unknown promised land of Canaan. The majority of your reading will come from Genesis, but you will also read passages from other books in the Old Testament, as well as the New Testament. The story of Abraham is a faith journey. As you read about this famous Patriarch's life, you will learn more about God, but I also suspect you will learn a little more about yourself.

Most of the lessons will take about thirty minutes to complete. Each unit is divided into five lessons, designed to be done on a daily basis, five days a week. You will benefit most from doing the lessons one at a time, giving yourself time to reflect upon each lesson before moving to the next one. Be sure to begin each session with prayer, asking God to speak specifically to you through the lesson. Make notes in the margins of anything you sense God is applying directly to a situation in your life. If you are doing this study with a group, your notes will make great discussion points when you get together to discuss your homework.

All quotations are from the New International Version of the Bible, unless otherwise noted. All Hebrew and Greek definitions are taken from *Strongs Exhaustive Concordance of the Bible* unless another source is listed.

Week 1

An Unprecedented Move

A Divine Directive

The LORD had said to Abram, "Go from your country, your people
and your father's household to the land I will show you."

GENESIS 12:1

braham is among the best-known men of the Bible. Whether you have studied the Scriptures for years or have never read a Bible on your own, you have probably heard of the Patriarch, Abraham. There is not a single book of the Bible that was written by Abraham; he did not speak any recorded prophesy; he was not a conqueror of kingdoms. Yet, Abraham is known as the Father of the Hebrew nation.

How does God describe Abraham in Isaiah 41:8? _____

On Sunday mornings at my home church, the praise band often performs a popular worship song that includes a chorus declaring God to be "a friend of mine." All that is within me desires to one day hear God graciously refer to me as His friend. But I cannot bring myself to declare it for myself. Instead, I stand in reverent silence as those words are sung and pray, *May it be so, Lord.* I can think of no greater reward in Heaven than for God to call me His friend. Abraham received that reward.

So, as we embark on this study based upon the life of Abraham, let's pause for a moment to pray that during the course of our time together, God will give us a better understanding of the relationship He and Abraham shared. For it is that relationship that prompted God to call Abraham His friend.

Write your prayer on the lines below:

_____

_____

_____

_____

Abraham's parents actually named him Abram. God later changed his name to Abraham (See Genesis 17:5). Abram means "Exalted Father."[1]

Please begin by reading Genesis 11:27-30.

What were the names of Abram's two brothers (vs.27)?_____ and _____

After the death of Haran, whom did Nahor marry and how were the two related?

_____

Whom did Abram marry and what detail do you learn from verse 30 that might have significantly impacted this man named Exalted Father?

_____

It occurs to me that whenever someone referred to Abram by name, they were reminding him of the children he lacked. God indeed had plans for Abram to eventually become an exalted father among his people, but as our study begins, Abram's circumstances gave no hint of the position that awaited him.

He and Sarai lived in a town named Ur. It was an important trade city along the Euphrates River in Southern Mesopotamia, located in what is now modern-day Iraq. It was a wealthy metropolis and its "citizens enjoyed a level of comfort unknown in other Mesopotamian cities."[2] Ur was also replete with the worship of many idols and false gods, which were believed to be ruled by a moon god, appropriately named "Sin."

> It occurs to me that whenever someone referred to Abram by name, they were reminding him of the children he lacked.

What does Joshua 24:2 tell you about Abram's father, Terah?

_____

In that culture, extended families lived together under one roof. It is safe to assume Abram was greatly influenced by his father and probably also worshipped the non-existent moon god named Sin. So Abram was living his life amid the comforts of a wealthy, thriving city, worshipping a false god he believed controlled the moon, when he received a startling message from the one true God—the God of all the heavens and all the earth (Genesis 24:3).

What was God's message to Abram, recorded in Genesis 12:1?

_____

_____

Pretend for a moment that you are in Abram's position. Your family has worshipped numerous gods your entire life. Suddenly, a God declaring Himself to be the one, true God speaks to you in a dream and instructs you to move out of your father's household and leave the country where you have lived your entire life. (Don't forget; you also have to leave behind all of your friends and your extended family members!) God tells you to leave and just travel around in other countries until He makes it clear where you and your immediate family are to settle and build a new home. What do you think would be the most difficult aspect of that request for you personally?

_____

Abram and Sarai were a real couple, deeply rooted in their affluent city of Ur. They probably regularly enjoyed the company of long-time friends, enjoyed a sense of security living with their extended family, and appreciated the perks that go along with living in a wealthy city. God asked a lot of Abram and Sarai. They were instructed to leave behind everything that was familiar and comfortable, to follow a God they probably knew little about, without having any idea where they were going. I would guess their struggles to obey God were similar to the difficulties you just wrote down.

Yet, what does Hebrews 11:8 tell you about Abram (Abraham)?

God interrupted Abram's predictable (and probably quite comfortable) life in the affluent city of Ur. Without having any idea where he and Sarai would end up, Abram left his home, simply because God instructed him to do so. As we will see, Abram took some unscheduled detours and made mistakes along his journey, but he eventually developed a strong, unwavering faith that prompted him to obey and trust in God's ability to keep His promises.

Read Hebrews 11:1 and summarize the definition of faith in your own words:

Obedience is the result of faith, and faith, in simplistic terms, means you believe what God says, regardless of your circumstances. Abram's decision to leave Ur was an act of obedience, prompted by faith that God is who He says He is and is able to do what He says He will do.

Our obedience is evidence of our faith. We can passionately sing God's praises during church worship services or quote appropriate passages of Scripture to fit every circumstance, but our willingness to obey God's commands and embrace the principles in His Word are evidence that confirms our faith.

> Obedience is the result of faith, and faith, in simplistic terms, means you believe what God says, regardless of your circumstances. Our obedience is evidence of our faith.

Like Abraham, it is when our sandals meet the rocky road of an unexpected divine directive that the true depth of our faith is revealed.

WEEK ONE | **DAY TWO**

Be a Blessing

"I will make you into a great nation, and I will bless you;
I will make your name great, and you will be a blessing."

GENESIS 12:2

Yesterday, Abram's not-so-ordinary life in the affluent trade city of Ur was interrupted as God instructed him to leave behind all that was familiar and comfortable to follow Him along an undefined path to a foreign land. Yet, that isn't all God said to Abram that day.

Please read Genesis 12:1-3 in your Bible.

Re-read verses 2-3 below from the NIV and underline every variation of the word "bless."

I will make you into a great nation, and I will bless you;
I will make your name great, and you will be a blessing.
I will bless those who bless you, and whoever curses you I will curse;
and all peoples on earth will be blessed through you.

Christians talk a lot about God's blessings. But the concept of being blessed seems vague, and as I read these passages, I found myself wondering exactly what God was promising the Patriarch. Let's do a little research and expand our understanding on the subject.

The word "blessing" is a common word with multiple, sometimes complex, meanings. For now, let's hone in on today's focus passages. The various forms of the word blessing that appear in Genesis 12:2-3 all originate from the same Hebrew word *barak*, which means "to kneel, or to bless" (Strongs). Interestingly, in order to receive the blessings God was promising, Abram was required to kneel, so to speak—to submit to God's plan and receive whatever God had for him. The word is used to describe the idea of God bestowing something good on people (or nature) or making them fruitful. The word can also be used to describe the way people can bless God by extolling Him in worship. "When we bless God, we bring His glories before our mind and respond in worship and adoration; when we ask Him to bless us, we invite Him to call our needs to mind and respond in meeting them."[3]

A blessing is not something we can control like our customized meals in a fast-food line. A blessing is received with a heart humbly yielded to God's purposes and plans, kneeling to receive whatever He chooses to give.

We have a tendency to maintain a narrow view of what constitutes a blessing. We consider ourselves blessed when our circumstances are easy or comfortable. However, a blessing is connected with God's kindness and goodness, experienced as we receive whatever God chooses to give us. We can be blessed, even in a time of great personal trial, when God responds to us with kindness and compassion amid our suffering. We can be blessed through a struggle as God increases our understanding of His power or gives us greater insight into our own weaknesses or prideful tendencies. We also experience a blessing when we become aware of God's active presence working in our personal circumstances in order to bring about something good or beneficial.

> Interestingly, in order to receive the blessings God was promising, Abram was required to kneel, so to speak—to submit to God's plan and receive whatever God had for him.

> A blessing is received with a heart humbly yielded to God's purposes and plans, kneeling to receive whatever He chooses to give.

To expand our thinking for a moment, let's mentally connect the word "blessing" with the concept of God working to do something good or beneficial through our circumstances. Are there any negative or difficult situations you have experienced, from which you have seen God eventually bring something good or beneficial? If so, briefly share the highlights below:

_____

_____

_____

The situation itself may not have been a blessing—in fact, it may have been tragic or even terrifying. But if you experienced God's faithfulness or kindness, or He brought about something beneficial or good from those terrible circumstances, you were blessed in some way, despite the circumstances of that event. Write your thoughts below:

_____

_____

Let's broaden our concept of a blessing a little further. Although God did promise to make Abram an abundant nation and give him a notable name, the ultimate purpose of the blessings God promised Abram appears to be the impact he would have upon "all peoples on earth."

Re-read Genesis 12:2-3.

In most translations of the Bible, we get the sense that God was predicting Abram would be a blessing (vs. 2). But the original language literally says, "Be a blessing."[4] God was basically saying, "I'm going to make you a great nation and your name will be honored for generations to come, so use your influence to make others aware of my kindness and goodness by being kind and generous toward others." In other words, "I'm going to bless you, so *be* a blessing."

He goes on to tell Abram that when he is indeed a blessing to others, those who respond with kindness toward Abram will receive kindness from God. And the best part? God said all people on earth would experience God's kindness and goodness through Abram.

According to the New International Encyclopedia of Bible Words, the word "kindness" in the Bible "indicates faithfulness to a relationship. To show kindness is to act in a loyal, loving way to a person."[5] A blessing is experienced in the context of relationship, which is what makes the kind, benevolent act meaningful to the recipient. We will delve deeper into the concept of God's blessings and His kindness toward His people a little later in our study. For now, ask God to help you develop a broader definition of His blessings than simply comfortable, feel-good situations or material possessions.

> Ask God to help you develop a broader definition of His blessings than simply comfortable, feel-good situations or material possessions.

To solidify what we've discussed today, let's re-write Genesis 12:2-3 to express our broader definition of a blessing. Fill in the blanks below with the words "kindness" and "goodness."

I will make you into a great nation, and I will [show my _____ and _____ to] *you;*

I will make your name great, and you will [show my _____ and
_____ to others].

I will [show _____ and _____ to] *those who* [show
_____ and _____ to] *you, and whoever curses you
I will curse;*

And all peoples on earth will [experience my _____ and
_____] *through you.*

How does this exercise expand your concept of the meaning of these verses?

_____

_____

Let's look at one more passage before we conclude our lesson. Continuing with the idea
that we experience God's kindness and goodness (receive a blessing) in order to share
God's kindness and goodness with others (be a blessing), please read 2 Corinthians 1:3-4.

What blessings does Paul describe receiving from God, and how was he suggesting we
could, in turn, be a blessing to others?

_____

_____

Now read 2 Corinthians 1:5-11.

Keeping our broad concept in mind, what are some of the blessings Paul describes in
these verses?

_____

_____

How could Paul's perspective on his suffering in the Province of Asia challenge the idea
that a blessing is simply a good or comfortable experience or the receipt of material
possessions?

_____

As Paul described, there are times in our lives when we are under great pressure "far beyond our ability to endure." Some of you, like Paul, have had days when you despaired even of life itself (vs. 8). But we experience God's kindness and goodness (a blessing) as we sense His comforting presence during a time of great heartache or loss. We are blessed by the favor granted to us as God chooses to answer prayers raised on our behalf by dear friends in the faith, as we are delivered from fear or addiction or persecution.

Blessings involve far more than simply comfortable circumstances, grateful children, or a sizable investment portfolio. A blessing from God is received in the context of a relationship with Him that enables us to discern His kindness and goodness as He works in the midst of life's circumstances to bring about something good or beneficial.

As we close, let's take God's words to Abram personally. As our Lord chooses to bless us, we too are called to *be a blessing* to everyone we encounter.

> Blessings involve far more than simply comfortable circumstances, grateful children, or a sizable investment portfolio.

WEEK ONE · DAY THREE

Compromising Companions

*Terah took his son Abram, his grandson Lot son of Haran,
and his daughter-in-law Sarai, the wife of his son Abram,
and together they set out from Ur of the Chaldeans to go to Canaan.*

GENESIS 11:31

Abram and Sarai had a clear directive from the Lord. It was time to pack up and leave behind their hometown of Ur. Scripture doesn't record the specifics of this departure. We don't have details of the exhausting task of packing up belongings or the emotional account of goodbyes spoken to long-time friends. As a matter of fact, Genesis chapter twelve dedicates only half a verse to what was probably a monumental act of faith on the part of Abram and his wife Sarai.

Genesis 12:4 simply says, "*So Abram went, as the LORD had told him; and Lot went with him.*"

Are you as surprised as I was to discover that Abram took Lot with him as he departed from his home in Ur?

According to Genesis 11:27, what was Lot's relationship to Abram?

_____

What command did God give Abram in Genesis 12:1 regarding his people and his father's household (in other words, his relatives)?

_____

Read Genesis 11:27-30 again. Can you think of any reasons Abram might have chosen to disobey God's instructions and take his nephew Lot with him when he left Ur?

_____

_____

_____

I wish I were there with you to hear your thoughts and talk this through while drinking cups of freshly brewed coffee and indulging on soft, chewy sugar cookies. There are no clear answers, but these passages offer a few clues about Abram's thought process. Obedience is never easy, and like Abram, there are situations we face every day that can make instructions from our Lord more challenging to follow.

Read Genesis 15:1-3. What disappointment did Abram express that might have influenced his decision to take his nephew along on his faith journey?

> Obedience is never easy, and like Abram, there are situations we face every day that can make instructions from our Lord more challenging to follow.

_____

Lot was without a father and Abram was without a son. I suspect Uncle Abram had become like a father to Lot. Abram's heartfelt cries to God in Genesis 15 make it clear he wanted a child. In fact, Abram couldn't think of any reward God could give him that would compare to the gift of having an heir. As Abram and Sarai prepared to follow God's directive, I imagine Abram probably rationalized, and even though God clearly told him to leave behind his people and the household of his father, Abram decided to take Lot along on his journey.

That isn't the only compromise Abram made as he exited Ur.

Please read Genesis 11:31. Who else accompanied Abram on his journey to the promised foreign land named Canaan?

_____

I got a kick out of the wording in this passage. It wasn't Abram who took Terah; it was Terah who took Abram. I get the sense Terah may have been a strong, controlling father. Those of you who have a strong, controlling father can probably write a script, detailing the conversation when Abram announced that he and Sarai were leaving Ur and didn't even know where they were going. I imagine Terah immediately began to take control, and before Abram could muster up the courage to defy his father's wishes, "Terah *took* his son Abram, his grandson Lot . . . and his daughter-in-law Sarai . . . and *together* they set out from Ur."

Family dynamics can be challenging, even in the best of situations, but during seasons of change, tempers can flare and emotions can become overwhelming. When obedience requires disappointing a parent or defying their wishes, even the most dedicated servants of God can waiver in their commitment to obey His commands.

Have you ever been in a situation where obeying God required you to disappoint a close friend or relative? If so, what compromises did you make or how did you maintain your commitment to obey God's directive? If you are doing this study with a group, consider sharing your answer at your next meeting.

> Have you ever been in a situation where obeying God required you to disappoint a close friend or relative?

_____

_____

_____

Interestingly, Abram made yet another compromise on his journey with God. Look again at Genesis 11:31. Where did this family, destined for Canaan, choose to settle instead?

_____

If you're like me, you are wondering why Abram would make such a choice. God was clear. Abram was supposed to leave his country and his family and travel until God showed him this mysterious unknown land.

If you recall, Ur was located in Mesopotamia on a trade route along the Euphrates River. Haran was also located in Mesopotamia, along another branch of the same river. Could it be that for a time, Abram settled for the familiar, rather than venturing away from a river that had probably been a source of food and security for his family throughout Abram's life?

My husband, Mark, and I live in Cypress, Texas, which is a part of the greater Houston area. I grew up in Southwest Houston. We raised our children in Northwest Houston. We have watched Houston grow and change over the years, but the familiar freeway system, the frustrating traffic patterns, and the predictably hot summers have been constants. I have many business and ministry connections from my years of work and service in the sprawling city. There is comfort and security in my familiar surroundings.

What familiar surroundings bring you a sense of comfort or security?

According to Acts 7:2-4, when did Abram finally leave Haran?

We don't know how many years Abram settled for the familiar, pleasing his earthly dad rather than following his heavenly Father, but we do know Abram waited until Terah died to follow God's directive and continue on to Canaan.

Perhaps Abram rationalized his decisions. He had obeyed God's command to leave Ur. Maybe he convinced himself he was simply making a scheduled stop and God was using Terah to direct his travels. Regardless, partial obedience is still disobedience, and there are usually consequences for disobedience.

> Partial obedience is still disobedience, and there are usually consequences for disobedience.

Read Genesis 12:4-7.

According to verse 7, what blessing did Abram experience once he finally arrived in Canaan?

The Lord appeared to Abram in Canaan. He promised to bless Abram in Canaan. By settling in Haran, Abram delayed far more than simply a visit to a foreign land. He delayed greater intimacy with God. Intimacy with our Lord is the greatest blessing we receive for our obedience to His commands.

> Intimacy with our Lord is the greatest blessing we receive for our obedience to His commands.

According to John 15:14, whom does Jesus call his friends?

If you are a follower of Jesus, your disobedience to God's commands doesn't negate your salvation. We can't earn eternal life. It is a free gift through faith in Christ. However, disobedience causes distance in our relationship with our Lord. When we settle for the familiar or choose to please people rather than follow God, we delay a deeper, more intimate relationship with Him that comes from walking closely with Him along life's sometimes rocky paths.

Abram was instructed to leave behind his country, his people, and his father's household. Yet, he chose to disobey some of God's commands and take his family along with him. As we will discover later in our study, compromise itself was a lingering companion of Abram's during the early years of his God-directed journey, but as the Patriarch's relationship with God deepened, he grew into a man of unwavering faith.

WEEK ONE   DAY FOUR

Unlikely Scenarios

The LORD appeared to Abram and said, "To your offspring I will give this land." So he built an altar there to the LORD, who had appeared to him.

GENESIS 12:7

When we last saw Abram, he and Sarai had finally arrived in Canaan, where Abram had a life-altering encounter with his Lord.

Please read Genesis 12:7 at the top of the page. What promise did God make to Abram during that encounter in Canaan?

_____

Now read the passages below and note what you learn about the land God promised to Abram's yet unborn offspring:

Deuteronomy 6:3 _____

Exodus 3:8 _____

God promised Abram's descendants a good, fruitful, and spacious land to one day call home. However, as Abram and Sarai entered that lush, fruitful land of promise for the first time, there wasn't anything in their surroundings that hinted of the land's association with a holy, righteous God. The Canaanites were inhabiting the region at that time. They were an immoral people, steeped in a culture of decadent idol worship. Water was scarce in the region, and the society was dependent upon winter rains to sustain crops. The principal deity of the Canaanites was a false god named Baal, thought to control storms, springs, and water. "Canaanites believed that the gods could be helped to bring about fertility of the soil if people fertilized one another in the places of worship. Every Canaanite sanctuary had its own prostitutes for that purpose,"[6] and the landscape included crude, graphic images related to the worship of those idols.

According to Genesis 12:6-7, at what landmark did God appear to Abram in Shechem?

_____

"Canaanites had shrines in groves of oak trees, and Moreh may have been one of their cult centers."[7] It must have been a strange experience for Abram when God chose to make an appearance in the very epicenter of that perverse culture. The Lord not only told Abram he had finally arrived at the appointed destination (perhaps an unlikely choice in Abram's mind), but God also said the land would one day belong to Abram's offspring.

Skip ahead for a moment. Abram was 100 years old when the offspring God promised was finally born (Romans 4:19). According to Genesis 17:17, how old was Sarah?

_____

About how old was Abram as he stood there in the presence of God at the great tree of Moreh at Shechem (Genesis 12:4)?

_____

If Abram was roughly seventy-five, Sarai was sixty-five. Prior to that moment in God's presence at the tree in Shechem, I would imagine Abram—the man named Exalted Father from Ur of the Chaldeans—had come to the conclusion he would never live up to his name and children were not going to be a part of his future.

> If Abram was roughly seventy-five, Sarai was sixty-five.

Read Genesis 12:6-8 again. Keeping Abram's circumstances and his surroundings in mind, what emotions do you think might have prompted Abram to call on the name of the Lord and build a second altar there near his tent?

_____

_____

Have you ever witnessed an amazing move of God in an unlikely location? My friend Richard Gillespie and his wife, Betty, certainly had that experience. He and his wife owned a Christian bookstore in the Houston, Texas, area. Their bookstore was my favorite place to purchase reference books because Richard knew the theology of the authors, the background of the publishers, and if I told him about something specific I was researching, he was almost always able to guide me to just the right resources. When the couple was searching for a new location for their bookstore, they prayed earnestly and searched tirelessly for a location that would enable them to continue serving the same community. However, there were limited retail spaces available, and finding a location within budget was challenging. However, God was faithful and an ideal location opened up, just down the road from their previous location. Imagine their surprise when they toured the space and discovered the tenant at the time was a skateboard and surfing store, also specializing in smoke and drug paraphernalia. As they sensed God confirming the new location for their store, Richard and Betty probably felt a lot like Abram must have felt that day when God announced that Canaan—the land riddled with Asherah poles and altars dedicated to sexually oriented worship practices—was the land Abram and Sarai's descendants would one day call home. But Richard and Betty prayed over every square foot of that lease space. They anointed it with oil and offered up the location as an offering to God before they moved their Christian Bookstore to that location. They faithfully served God and the community in that location until they retired.

> Have you ever witnessed an amazing move of God in an unlikely location?

Interestingly, many years after Abram's encounter with God at Shechem, as his descendants, called the Israelites, prepared to take possession of that rich land promised to the Patriarch, God described how He planned to redeem the land of Canaan and turn it into a place where His holy and chosen people would live as His treasured possession.

Please read God's instructions as recorded in Deuteronomy 7:1-6.

According to verse 1, who would drive out the people inhabiting the land, including the Canaanites?

_____

Why were the Israelites warned not to intermarry with the Canaanites or let them stay in the land (vs. 4)?

_____

What were God's people supposed to do to the Canaanites' altars and Asherah poles?

_____

I imagine as Abram traveled through the land, he continued processing God's promises. He pitched his tent between Bethel and Ai and felt compelled to build a second altar to honor his God. As Abram called upon the name of the Lord, I wonder if he asked God to cleanse the land, to bless his descendants, and to protect them while they lived there. I would also guess Abram also thanked God in advance for all He intended to do for His people in that place.

> As Abram called upon the name of the Lord, I wonder if he asked God to cleanse the land, to bless his descendants, and to protect them while they lived there.

As the sun set over that second, freshly built altar, Abram must have been overwhelmed with the goodness of God and the enormity of those promises. The future Exalted Father might have expected to settle down there in Canaan and begin his new life with Sarai. But the Canaanites were occupying the good, fertile land, and it wasn't time for God to drive them out. Therefore, Genesis 12:9 tells us Abram set out for the Negev, which was a barren, desert region of Canaan.

> As the sun set over that second, freshly built altar, Abram must have been overwhelmed with the goodness of God and the enormity of those promises.

Abram had arrived in the foreign land God promised to show him (Genesis 12:1), but I doubt Canaan was what Abram had in mind when he and Sarai left their hometown on faith. Once there, the couple didn't find a new, comfortable home with the luxuries they left behind in the wealthy city of Ur. The closest they had come to calling Canaan home was the tent they had pitched _between_ cities—a scenario Abram could never have anticipated.

Read 1 Corinthians 1:27-29 and note why God often works through unlikely people and unexpected scenarios.

_____

God chose a barren, elderly couple to be the birth parents of a people group through which He would bless the entire world. Our Lord chose a country riddled with idols and perverse worship practices to be the land His beloved people would one day call home. Unlikely scenarios were going to be commonplace in the lives of Abram and Sarai. I doubt there was even a hint of boasting as the couple said goodbye to the lush, fruitful land of Canaan and headed into Negev, unless, of course, they were boasting about the kindness and goodness of their Lord.

> God chose a barren, elderly couple to be the birth parents of a people group through which He would bless the entire world.

WEEK ONE DAY FIVE

Personal Application

*E*ach week you will spend your fifth day of study reflecting upon the material you covered in the previous four lessons. I encourage you to use this format to review and gain additional insight that will help you apply what you are learning to your everyday life.

Application from Day 1

In Day One this week, Abram was going about his usual routine in the wealthy Mesopotamian city of Ur, worshipping a God he believed controlled the moon, when he received a divine directive from the one true God of all the heavens and all the earth. God instructed Abram to leave his country, his people, and his father's household (Genesis 12:1) and go to an unknown foreign land. Hebrews 11:8 tells us Abram "obeyed and went, even though he did not know where he was going."

To refresh your memory, how does God describe Abram (later named Abraham) in Isaiah 41:8?

_____

> Hebrews 11:8 tells us Abram "obeyed and went, even though he did not know where he was going."

Read John 15:13-15. Who is it that Jesus considers His friends?

_____

In Jesus, all the fullness of God came to earth in bodily form (Colossians 2:9). Anyone who has seen Jesus has seen the Father (John 14:9), so if Jesus considers friends those who choose to obey His commands, then the depth of our relationship with God is also revealed by our commitment to the commands of His Word. Obedience isn't required for salvation. We are saved by grace through faith (Ephesians 2:8). However, obedience is important as we seek to develop a relationship with our God. Read each of the following passages and note what you learn about God's perspective regarding our obedience to His commands:

1 Samuel 15:22: _____

> Obedience is important as we seek to develop a relationship with our God. God desires for us to obey His commands because in so doing, we can persevere through the storms of life.

_____

Psalm 128:1: _____

_____

Luke 6:46-49: _____

_____

God desires for us to obey His commands because in so doing, we can persevere through the storms of life. His commands are for our good. They are not an oppressive list of rules. In God's Word, we discover true security and intimacy with our God. Our monetary offerings are important and honored by God, but when we are willing to sacrifice our desires or give up our rights in order to live out the commands of God's Word, when we choose to display Christ-like love to another person, we are revealing the depth of our faith and our love for our God.

According to Hebrews 11:6, why is faith required to please God?

_____

As I said in our opening lesson, I can think of no greater reward in heaven than to hear our God refer to us as His friends.

Application from Day 2

In Day Two we explored the meaning of the word "blessing" and the concept of being blessed by God. We connected the idea of a blessing to the awareness of God's kindness and goodness expressed by His work to bring about something good or beneficial from our circumstances.

Read Romans 8:28-29. According to verse 29, what is God's overall purpose for every believer in Christ?

_____

Think about your circumstances, good or bad, over the past month. How do you think God might be blessing you by using your situation to conform you more fully into the image of His Son? (If you are doing this study with a small group, take some time to talk about this as a group.)

> How do you think God might be blessing you by using your situation to conform you more fully into the image of His Son?

Application from Day 3

In our Day Three lesson this week, Abram compromised his commitment to God's instructions. Read each of the commands God gave Abram as recorded in Genesis 12:1 and note how Abram compromised. Try to write your answers from memory, but look back at Day Three's lesson for help, if needed.

God told Abram to

1). Leave his country. Compromise: _____

_____

2). Leave his people. Compromise: _____

_____

3). Leave his father's household. Compromise: _____

_____

To which of these compromises of Abram do you most relate and why?

_____

_____

These are the first of many compromises we will see Abram make on his journey with God. As we move forward with the study, ask God to reveal to you any tendencies of Abram's with which you sometimes struggle. I pray we can learn from the compromises in our protagonist's story. Thankfully, he eventually grew into a man of unwavering faith.

> Ask God to reveal to you any tendencies of Abram's with which you sometimes struggle.

Application from Day 4

Unlikely scenarios will prove to be commonplace in the lives of Abram and Sarai. In fact, God often does some of His greatest work through people with the fewest qualifications. He often chooses the "foolish things of the world to shame the wise" (1 Corinthians 1:27). As you follow God along your life's journey, like Abram, circumstances will rarely be what you expect or anticipate.

Read 1 Corinthians 1:27-29 again. Why do you think boasting with a sense of superiority or having an inflated concept of our own importance (in other words, pride) might be counter-productive to an intimate relationship with our Lord?

_____

Read the following verses and note the damage that results from pride.

Deuteronomy 8:10-14 _____

Psalm 10:4 _____

Pride is destructive to our relationship with our God because we tend to forget Him when we believe we are self-sufficient. Today's society is rampant with selfies, self-help books, and a sense of self-entitlement. Most Americans are wealthy compared with people in many countries across our globe. If we are not careful, we can fall into the trap of believing we are entitled to the comforts and perks America provides. We can forget our God and come to the conclusion we are self-made and self-sustained. God planned to bless all nations through Abram. The wandering future patriarch needed to remember the source of those blessings. As with Abraham, God blesses in order that we may be a blessing. As we close this week, once again ask God to help you be a blessing to everyone you encounter along your life's journey.

> Pride is destructive to our relationship with our God because we tend to forget Him when we believe we are self-sufficient.

Week 2

Compromising Conditions

Self-seeking Ruse

Truthful lips will be established forever,
but a lying tongue is [credited] only for a moment.

PROVERBS 12:19 AMP

When we last saw Abram and Sarai, they were in a barren desert region called the Negev. The fruitful, lush Promised Land was behind them, and the couple was probably feeling a bit homesick as they tried to embrace their new nomadic lifestyle. As if they had not already endured enough change, circumstances continued to grow more challenging for the future patriarch and his less-than-youthful bride.

Please read Genesis 12:10-13.

If we were watching this unfold on a movie screen, the scene we just read would be accompanied by dramatic background music, alerting us to danger lurking ahead in the storyline. I'm touched by Abram's awareness of his sixty-five-year-old wife's beauty, even after many years of marriage. However, the comment becomes less endearing when you consider Abram's thoughtful focus upon his own well-being and lack of concern for the possible ramifications his ruse might bring for Sarai.

Now, technically speaking, Abram's suggestion that Sarai refer to herself as his sister wasn't entirely false. In Genesis 20:12, how does Abram say he and his wife are related?

Now, I do not see any indication in the text that Abram asked God what he should do when faced with a famine in the Negev. After building two altars and calling on the name of the Lord in the fertile areas of Canaan, Abram appears to have depended upon his own instincts when faced with a famine in the desert. Rather than consulting the Lord, he resorted to deception as he considered the possible opposition in Egypt.

Before you are too hard on old Abe, consider how you have reacted to uncertainty or adverse circumstances recently. Did you immediately seek God and His counsel, or did you find yourself concocting your own plan for self-preservation? Write your thoughts below:

Regardless of your answer, there is much we can learn from Abram's decision to deceive the Egyptians. It is sometimes easy to convince ourselves we are not lying when we offer partial information, such as Abram telling the Egyptians Sarai was his sister. However, omitting the important fact that Sarai was also Abram's wife was a lie. A lie is "a false statement made with deliberate intent to deceive; an intentional untruth; a falsehood."[8]

> It is sometimes easy to convince ourselves we are not lying when we offer partial information, such as Abram telling the Egyptians Sarai was his sister.

One time when our son was in high school, he told me he was going to a classmate's house after school and made a point to mention that the friend's mother would be home. That was true. But he failed to tell me his friend's mother was setting up a place in her garage where the boys could smoke. He did not technically tell a lie, but he implied that the presence of the mother would ensure nothing improper would be going on. In other words, it was an attempt to deceive by simply leaving out an important piece of information because Brandon knew his dad and I would not approve. When we discovered the deception, let's just say punishment was swift.

Abram's intent was to give the false impression that he and Sarai were merely a brother and sister travelling together. Simply stated, Abram asked Sarai to lie to the Egyptians so they would treat *him* well.

Read Proverbs 12:19 from the Amplified Bible at the beginning of this lesson and note what it tells us about lying. (Insert the dramatic background music once again.)

WEEK TWO

Let's see how Abram's reckless plan unfolded. Please read Genesis 12:14-20.

Sarai was taken into the palace to become a member of Pharaoh's harem, and I would guess Abram's guilt grew and his distress increased with each sheep, donkey, camel, and servant he received from the enamored king. And Sarai? She probably became more indignant every morning she woke up in that Egyptian palace.

> God may not have been consulted, but Abram's rash plan did not escape His attention.

God may not have been consulted, but Abram's rash plan did not escape His attention. According to verse 17, what did God do and to whom did He do it?

When everyone in the palace became ill, with the exception of Sarai, Pharaoh wanted answers, and the historian Josephus indicates the inflicted king asked Sarai for an explanation.[9] Sarai's words are not recorded in Scripture, but she apparently made the situation perfectly clear because the angry king did not even ask for an explanation from Abram. Pharaoh simply told his men to send Abram and Sarai on their way with all of their belongings, including the livestock and servants the Egyptian king had given to Abram.

Read Genesis 13:1-2.

To where did Abram and Sarai return, and who went along with them?

What additional fact do you learn about Abram from verse 2?

Abram had gone down to Egypt without consulting God and walked away a wealthier man. However, he almost lost his beloved wife, Sarai. His self-seeking ruse had backfired. I would guess the trip from Egypt back to the Negev was marked by tension between the future patriarch and Sarai. After all, the couple had embarked on their divinely directed journey *together*. They had sacrificed the comforts of their former life in Ur *together*. Abram and Sarai probably dreamed of God's promised descendants *together*. Yet, when their travels brought them to a place of potential danger, Abram put their future together at risk in an attempt to save his own skin.

According to verses 3-4, where did the couple and their nephew return, and what did Abram do once again in that place?

_____

_____

Have you ever gotten off track in your journey with God? When I have found myself in the middle of a self-made mess, void of the joy and peace that comes from walking closely with my Lord, the best way I have found to restore order and get back on track is to return to the last place along my journey where I clearly sensed God's presence and experienced His peace.

Now, I think it is interesting that, according to Strong's Exhaustive Concordance, the Hebrew word translated *Bethel* means House of God, and the word translated *Ai* comes from a root word that means a ruin or a heap. So as Abram called upon the Lord afresh at that altar, he found himself right between the house of God and a heap of ruins. He could choose to seek God and be a blessing, just as God had commanded him. But Abram could also continue to follow his own instincts as he had in Egypt and end up with his dreams piled in a heap of ruins.

> Have you ever gotten off track in your journey with God? As Abram called upon the Lord afresh at that altar, he found himself right between the house of God and a heap of ruins.

Like Abram, when we have strayed from God's path or when our self-seeking ruses leave our relationships in a heap of ruins, let's seek God afresh. Let's commit to return to the safety of the House of our God. In fact, if I had been in Abram's situation, I might have moved my tent and built a new altar in Bethel, just to signify my desire to remain in the House of God.

As a way of closing today, read Ecclesiastes 5:1-2 and note how you should approach the house of God.

Take a moment to sit quietly before our Lord. Thankfully, when you get off track and return to Bethel, you do not need to approach God with a lengthy explanation. He is in heaven and you are on earth. He already knows the whole story. So let your words be few.

WEEK TWO | DAY TWO

A Quarrelling Caravan

And quarreling arose between Abram's herders and Lot's.
The Canaanites and Perizzites were also living in the land at that time.

GENESIS 13:7

Abram and Sarai were back in the Negev after their harrowing experience in Egypt. Abram had returned to the Promised Land and renewed his commitment to God's plan for his family. Speaking of family, Abram's favored nephew, Lot, may have been quiet during the debacle in Egypt, but he was still travelling with Uncle Abram and Aunt Sarai.

Let's see how the family road trip was going. Please read Genesis 13:5-7.

What fact stated in verse 7 explains why the land was unable to support both men's flocks and herds at this time?

In order to eventually take possession of the land, Abram's descendants would have to drive out the Canaanites and Perizzites, but those battles would not take place until many years later. So, as the two wealthy men moved about with their animals, possessions, and servants, the living conditions became overcrowded, and tempers began to flare.

Please read Genesis 13:8-13. What was Abram's proposed solution to their problem?

_____

According to verses 9-10, who had the first choice of land?

_____

In essence, Abram said, "You choose whatever land you want, Lot. I will go find a place to settle in the opposite direction." What does verse 10 tell you about the area Lot chose for himself?

_____

_____

As you consider Abram's offer and Lot's choice, what do you learn about the character of each of these men?

Abram: _____

Lot: _____

Abram was Lot's uncle. He was the head of the family. Not to mention, God had promised to give the land to Abram's descendants, and Lot was not one of them. Yet, Lot looked around and noticed the green pastures near Sodom and "chose for himself the whole plain of the Jordan." Rather than leaving the best land for his uncle, who had disobeyed God's instructions by allowing Lot to tag along on this God-ordained trip in the first place, the self-centered nephew took what appeared to be the best land for himself.

Interestingly, the situation between Abram and Lot not only provides insight into the nature of each of these men, it also reminds us that partial obedience to God's commands is still disobedience, and disobedience brings

> Interestingly, the situation between Abram and Lot not only provides insight into the nature of each of these men, it also reminds us that partial obedience to God's commands is still disobedience.

consequences. I have to wonder if one of the reasons God told Abram to leave his family behind is because the land could not support a multi-family caravan at this time. By taking Lot along with him to Canaan, Abram made his journey more difficult than necessary, and eventually, Abram recognized that he and Sarai needed to leave Lot behind.

What does Proverbs 3:11-12 tell us God does for those He loves?

The loving discipline of our Lord often comes in the form of some mighty uncomfortable circumstances. For Abram, it was a massive caravan of grumpy herders and servants. Abram may have recognized his error, but Lot appears to have been oblivious to the lesson. He made a selfish choice. But, our God is omniscient, which is a fancy way of saying He knows all things—past, present, and future.

> The loving discipline of our Lord often comes in the form of some mighty uncomfortable circumstances.

When God told Abram to leave Ur, He knew the land of Canaan could not support all of the possessions of both Lot and Abram; He knew Abram would take Lot anyway; He knew Abram would be overly gracious and allow Lot to choose where he wanted to settle; He knew Lot would be greedy and choose the well-watered land east of Canaan. Our God is also sovereign, which is another fancy word that means He is the supreme authority and has control over the ultimate outcome of events.

According to Ephesians 1:11, what is God able to do?

What does God say about Himself in Isaiah 46:9-11?

> Our omniscient, sovereign God knew full well what would take place between Abram and Lot there along the border of Canaan.

For whatever reasons, Lot was not supposed to be with Abram in Canaan. Although we struggle to understand how God can know and control circumstances yet still allow people to make their own choices, the fact is, our Lord is able to accomplish His purposes. He knows our strengths as well as our weaknesses. Before we speak a word, God already knows what we are going to say (Psalm 139:4). Our omniscient, sovereign God knew full well what would take place between Abram and Lot there along the border of Canaan.

EYEWITNESS TO PROMISE: ABRAHAM

When Abram said goodbye to his nephew and went to live in Canaan, he finally settled into a place of complete obedience to God's command to leave his country, his people, and his father's household.

Lot pitched his tents near Sodom. What does verse 13 tell us about the people of Sodom?

As Lot drifted off to sleep in his tent that night, I can once again imagine that familiar dramatic music strumming in the background as the screen fades to black. Trouble was ahead for Lot.

In contrast, Abram was right where God called him to be as he looked around at the vast land that would become known as the Promised Land. He was probably a little sad as he watched his nephew's caravan head off to the east. After all, Lot was the closest thing Abram had to a son. Interestingly, it was at that moment—as Abram stood obediently in the land of promise with just his wife and all of their earthly possessions— that God chose to speak to Abram once again.

Let's see what God had to say to Abram. Please read Genesis 13:14-18.

What did God once again promise Abram, and what new detail did He share with Abram about his future offspring?

God knew Abram's greatest desire was to have a son. I'm touched by His timing. As Abram grieved the loss of his son-like companion, God chose to tell Abram his offspring would one day be too numerous to count. Then our Lord told Abram to take a long walk through the land because it would all belong to his family.

Has God ever made His presence particularly real to you during a time of great loss? If so, briefly describe the circumstances and share how God comforted you during that time.

> God knew Abram's greatest desire was to have a son.

According to verse 18, where did Abram decide to settle after his walk through the "length and breadth" of the land?

I can't help but wonder if Abram intentionally kicked up dust as he walked through the land that day. He decided to settle among some trees in the southern area of Canaan in a town named Hebron. I imagine Abram and Sarai talked about God's promised offspring as they cleaned the dust off their feet and prepared to settle into their tent for that evening. He had parted ways with a son-like nephew but fell asleep with the assurance he would one day have countless descendants of his own.

WEEK TWO **DAY THREE**

Consequential Rescue

They also carried off Abram's nephew Lot and his possessions,
since he was living in Sodom.

GENESIS 14:12

Abram and Sarai were finally in a place of complete obedience to God's call. They had indeed left behind their hometown of Ur and its people; they had severed ties with Abram's relatives and were following God in the land of Canaan. The couple found a place to call home near the great trees of Mamre in Hebron, located in the southeast region of Canaan. Once their tents were set up, Abram's first order of business was to build an altar to the Lord. He then worshipped the one true God as he and his bride began a new life together.

Abram and Lot each settled into their new surroundings. In the course of time, the consequences for Lot's self-serving decision to make his home near the wicked city of Sodom began to play out when a battle started brewing between kings in the area, including the rulers of Sodom and Gomorrah. Read Genesis 14:1-12.

If you are like me, you struggled to picture this scene as you muddled your way through the names and locations of the various, unfamiliar kings. I attempted to gather some interesting data that would help bring these passages to life. However, if the kings mentioned here were interesting, their accomplishments have eluded me. So, in order to move forward with our storyline, let's just settle for a big-picture understanding of these events.

Four kings had dominated five kings in the region for twelve years. In the thirteenth year, the five lesser kings rebelled. In the year that followed, the four stronger kings conquered a lot of territory in the region, and in the fourteenth year, the five lesser kings came together to take a stand. However, things did not go so well for the five lesser kings, which included the kings of Sodom and Gomorrah.

What happened to the men of Sodom and Gomorrah as they fled during the battle (vs. 10)?

_____

Who did the winning kings seize during the battle (vs. 12)? _____

According to Genesis 14:13, how was Abram made aware that his nephew was in trouble?

_____

How is Abram described in this verse? _____

Interestingly, this is the first time anyone in Scripture is referred to as a Hebrew. The name may be related to a term that meant "To cross over (from the other side),"[10] and reflected the people's awareness that Abram came from across the Euphrates.

Many years later, Abram's descendants became slaves to the reigning Pharaoh in Egypt. If you are familiar with Scripture, you know that God sent Moses to deliver Abram's descendants from slavery. How does Moses describe God to Pharaoh in Exodus 5:3?

_____

Unlike the other people in Canaan, Abram worshipped one holy, pure God who created and ruled both heaven and earth. Abram was from the other side of the tracks, so to speak, and his worship wasn't accompanied by the depraved practices of the Canaanites. Abram was a Hebrew, and the way he worshipped and lived his life was distinctive from his neighbors. But rather than being considered an enemy invading their territory, Abram appears to have gained his

> Unlike the other people in Canaan, Abram worshipped one holy, pure God who created and ruled both heaven and earth.

neighbors' respect and support. He befriended Mamre and his brothers, Eshkol and Aner, and people in the region evidently knew Abram and cared enough about his family to alert him of his nephew's capture. Let's see what happened next. Please read Genesis 14:14-16.

What did Abram do upon hearing the news?

_____

_____

Abram could have let his nephew, Lot, endure whatever consequences his life choices brought his way. Yet, the future patriarch chose to risk his own well-being to help his self-centered nephew. I imagine Abram said a quick prayer for Lot and his family. However, it is clear he didn't stop there. The concerned uncle sprang into action.

How are Abram's 318 men described (vs. 14)?

_____

_____

The four kings involved in this battle had dominated the region for years. They were a strong force. Abram was not a military man. Yet, he still made sure the men in his household were trained and prepared to defend their camp from threats. Now his nephew was in trouble and their preparation would serve them well. Abram chose to trust God and take action. He chose to lead his men, along with his allies Mamre, Eshkol, and Aner (vs. 13), into battle against the strong kings' armies by faith. The 318 trained men pursued Lot's captors about 140 miles north to a territory later named Dan.

> With God's help, the small army led by the outsider from across the river defeated the armies of four powerful kings. After all, Abram had God on his side.

During the night, Abram devised a plan to seal the victory. He divided his men up and attacked from multiple directions, catching the enemy by surprise, chasing them about 100 miles further north to Hobah.[11] With God's help, the small army led by the outsider from across the river defeated the armies of four powerful kings. After all, Abram had God on his side.

What does the psalmist declare about God in Psalm 18:27-29?

_____

_____

Look closely at Genesis 14:16. What appears to have been Abram's only purpose for this battle?

_____

_____

Abram didn't take anything that belonged to those defeated cities. He wasn't interested in conquering kingdoms or taking possession of their land. After all, look back at Genesis 12:7. What promise did God make to Abram regarding the land?

Abram was walking by faith. God's promise was all the evidence Abram needed that this land would one day be his. He did not need to stake claims or conquer kingdoms. Abram had God's promise. This military campaign was simply a recovery operation, but, in the process, they defeated five cities. Can you imagine the amount of pottery, gold, and jewelry that must have been taken from five cities? Abram probably had all 318 men, along with every woman and child recovered in the battle, hauling items back home.

> Abram was walking by faith. God's promise was all the evidence Abram needed that this land would one day be his.

Once Abram was safely back in Canaan, he had a couple of intriguing visitors. Please read Genesis 14:17-24.

What surprising visitor was first to arrive? _____

According to verse 21, what did the king offer to let Abram keep?

Now, I find this exchange interesting. This king had been dominated and defeated by the very group of kings Abram had just conquered. Whatever spoils Abram brought back from the battle would rightly be his anyway. The king of Sodom was not in a position to offer Abram anything except, perhaps, his gratitude. How did Abram respond to the king's offer (vs. 22-24)?

Abram did not want any of it. He was not about to give the king of Sodom the satisfaction of thinking he was the source of Abram's wealth. What oath had Abram taken to God before he ever entered into battle (Genesis 14:22-23)?

The gracious leader compensated his companions with a share for their efforts, but he did not keep any of the recovered goods for himself. Abram knew he was not a self-made man, but he was going to make sure no one thought he was a king-of-Sodom-made man. Abram put action to his faith and rescued his nephew. Before we move forward with our story, tomorrow we will explore the significance of Abram's second mysterious visitor that day. Melchizedek's presence served to remind Abram that he was a God-made man.

> Abram put action to his faith and rescued his nephew.

WEEK TWO | DAY FOUR

A Mysterious Visitor

This Melchizedek was king of Salem and priest of God Most High.
He met Abraham returning from the defeat of the kings and blessed him.

HEBREWS 7:1

When we last saw Abram, he told the king of Sodom to keep the goods retrieved in battle and made it clear he was not about to let the king take credit for the wealth God had graciously bestowed upon him. But there was also a second, more intriguing, man who visited Abram that day.

To refresh your memory, please read Genesis 14:17-20.

According to verse 18, what two titles did Melchizedek hold?

_____ and _____

Please read Hebrews 7:1-4.

According to verse 2, what does the name Melchizedek mean?

_____

What does the name king of Salem mean? _____

What else do these passages reveal about this mysterious priest?

_____

_____

_____

How long would Melchizedek remain a priest (vs. 3)? _____

This priest and king of Salem was what is called a type—a prediction or a picture representing something or someone who would come later. In this case, Melchizedek was a type of Jesus Christ—the King of Righteousness and the Prince of Peace.

> This priest and king of Salem was what is called a type— a prediction or a picture representing something or someone who would come later.

To clarify, the description of Melchizedek being without father or mother or genealogy does not mean he was an angel or that he appeared out of nowhere. A priest is chosen from among people (Hebrews 5:1), and angels do not serve as priests. These passages simply mean Melchizedek's origin is not recorded anywhere because his priesthood was not established on the basis of his heritage.[12] He was a priest appointed by God and his priesthood would last forever.

The Lord would later establish a priesthood for Abram's descendants. These priests would collect tithes and offerings, oversee and care for the temple, and offer sacrifices on behalf of the people. The men who would hold these priestly positions descended from an Israelite named Levi, and only his descendants could be priests. Levitical priests served for a maximum of 25 years (Numbers 8:24-25). Their sacrifices brought temporary forgiveness for sins, but the animal sacrifices had to be offered regularly, according to specific guidelines, and they never actually removed sins. We will explore this further later in our study, but the Levitical priesthood illustrated the work of Christ, who, as the Messiah, would one day come and take away the sins of the entire world for all time.

We learn something distinctive about Melchizedek's priesthood during his meeting with Abram. Look back at Genesis 14:18. How is God described in this verse?

_____

This is the first time this particular name for God is used in Scripture. In Hebrew, the name is *El Elyon*. It is a universal name for God that represents Him "as possessor of heaven and earth, and God above all national...distinctions."[13] The Most High God (*El Elyon*) emphasizes the fact that God is sovereign over all people and nations.

The Levitical priests descended from Abram and only functioned as priests for the people of Israel. Melchizedek, in contrast, was a priest of The Most High God, El Elyon. He was priest for people of all nations, and his priestly order would last forever.

> Melchizedek was a priest of The Most High God, El Elyon. He was priest for people of all nations, and his priestly order would last forever.

Look back at God's promise to Abram in Genesis 12:3. Who did God say would be blessed through him?

This visit from Melchizedek was a shadowy glimpse of what was ahead. Through Abram's descendants, all nations would be blessed, and the priesthood of Melchizedek was established for all people. This lesson is a little tedious, but stay with me as we connect all of this information.

Psalm 110 is a prophetic psalm that points to the coming Messiah who would be king and a priest. That Messiah is our Jesus. According to Psalm 110:4, how long will King Jesus be a priest and from what priestly order?

> Psalm 110 is a prophetic psalm that points to the coming Messiah who would be king and a priest. That Messiah is our Jesus.

According to Hebrews 4:14, what type of priestly role does Jesus hold?

Now read Hebrews 5:1-6.

Why did Levitical priests have to offer sacrifices for their own sins as well as for the sins of the people (vs. 2-3)?

Who appointed Jesus as high priest (vs. 5)? _____

Now read Hebrews 7:23-27. What is distinctive about our eternal high priest, Jesus?

_____

_____

Read Romans 5:1 from The Amplified Bible below:

> *Therefore, since we are justified (acquitted, declared righteous, and given a right standing with God) through faith, let us [grasp the fact that we] have [the peace of reconciliation to hold and to enjoy] peace with God through our Lord Jesus Christ (the Messiah, the Anointed One).*

Now look back at the meaning of Melchizedek's names. How did this mysterious priest who met with Abraham reflect the standing we have before God through faith in Jesus?

_____

The mysterious king and priest who visited Abram does not make another appearance in Scripture. He was a king and priest of God Most High, representing the King of Kings and the Prince of Peace, who would one day sacrifice Himself so that all people on earth could be blessed with right standing (righteousness) and peace with God.

As a way of closing, take a moment to thank God for the righteousness and peace you have through faith in Jesus.

The fruit of that righteousness will be peace; its effect will be quietness and confidence forever.
—Isaiah 32:17

WEEK TWO | **DAY FIVE**

Personal Application

Application from Days One and Two

In the Day One lesson, Abram and Sarai encountered a famine in the Negev, and, rather than seeking God for guidance, the couple went to Egypt where Abram, concerned Pharaoh would try to kill him in order to take Sarai as one of his wives, told the Egyptian king he and Sarai were simply brother and sister.

> Proceeding from instinct rather than seeking God's counsel becomes a pattern in Abram's life. Many of us make the same mistake when faced with uncertainty.

Abram reacted to a hardship and potential danger by relying upon his natural instincts rather than seeking divine guidance. In fact, proceeding from instinct rather than seeking God's counsel becomes a pattern in Abram's life. Many of us make the same mistake when faced with uncertainty.

What do the following passages reveal about the importance of seeking God when we feel threatened or our circumstances seem uncertain?

Psalm 32:8-10: _____

Proverbs 3:5-6: _____

James 1:5: _____

At this stage in Abram's journey with God, he relied upon his own understanding rather than seeking counsel and wisdom from God. In fact, he had disobeyed God by bringing his nephew Lot to the land of Canaan. As is usually the case, that disobedience brought consequences. Abram and Lot's herders began arguing. But look closely at Genesis 13:8. Who else may have been arguing as a result of the overcrowding in Canaan?

One truth I have learned (the hard way!) is that if we are not willing to obey God initially, our consequences often become uncomfortable enough that we obey Him eventually. What about you? Has God ever used uncomfortable or painful circumstances to discipline you and bring you back to a place of obedience to His Word? If so, what did *you* learn from that experience?

_____

_____

As Abram grows and his relationship with God deepens, he will learn to seek counsel and wisdom from God. Let's learn from Abram and avoid the consequences and discomfort that usually follow when we make decisions based upon our own understanding.

> If we are not willing to obey God initially, our consequences often become uncomfortable enough that we obey Him eventually. Let's learn from Abram and avoid the consequences and discomfort that usually follow when we make decisions based upon our own understanding.

Application from Day Three

Abram did not appear to have any interest in conquering kingdoms or staking claims to land. Yet, when his nephew was kidnapped by a group of ruthless kings, Abram rallied his men and bravely fought to bring Lot back home.

Look back at Genesis 14:14. How are the men Abram took into battle described?

_____

Abram was just living his life and following God. He was not a military man and seems to have made far more friends than he did enemies. Yet, the servants in his household were trained to defend the camp and fight if necessary.

> Every believer in Christ has a spiritual enemy from whom we must defend ourselves.

Maybe you are a peaceful soul yourself, and you would prefer to avoid conflict and focus your attention on sharing the love of Christ and serving God with passion. However, the truth is, every believer in Christ has a spiritual enemy from whom we must defend ourselves. Training is essential to live the victorious life God intends for His people.

According to 1 Peter 5:8, who is a Christian's enemy, and why should we be alert and prepared for battle?

_____

Read Ephesians 6:10-18.

Although it is easy to forget, our struggle is not against other people. According to verse 12, with whom do we struggle?

_____

What does our spiritual armor equip us to do (vs. 11)?

_____

According to verse 18, what do we need to do in order to be effective in battle, and how often should we do it?

_____

Our battle is against the spiritual forces of evil that influence people and manipulate circumstances in an effort to knock us down and hinder our ability to serve and honor God. When we cover ourselves with the spiritual armor provided for us through faith in Christ, we are able to withstand our enemy's schemes.

Look again at the list of armor in Ephesians 6:13-17. The belt of truth means we have an understanding of spiritual truths and we are honest in our dealings. Our breastplate is the knowledge that we are considered righteous in God's sight through faith in Jesus. Having our feet covered in readiness means we have a basic understanding of the gospel and know we are at peace with God. Our shield, faith, is the ability to trust God, even when we don't understand our circumstances. The helmet of salvation is our assurance that we truly are saved through faith in Christ. And finally, our sword of the spirit is a solid understanding of God's Word that equips us to reject the lies of our enemy.

> When we cover ourselves with the spiritual armor provided for us through faith in Christ, we are able to withstand our enemy's schemes. Spend some time talking about how you can shore up your spiritual armor.

Look through the list again. What pieces of armor do you have firmly in place and where do you need a little more training?

I wear these often: _____

I am vulnerable here: _____

Like Abram's men, we should be preparing ourselves for battle (studying the Bible and deepening our relationship with our Lord) before a threat comes our way. If you are doing this study with a group, spend some time talking about how you can shore up your spiritual armor. Make notes below. If you are studying by yourself, spend some time in prayer and write your thoughts below:

_____

_____

Application from Day Four

Melchizedek is a type—a shadow and picture of Jesus Christ, our King and appointed High Priest. Read Hebrews 4:14-16.

According to verse 15, why is Jesus able to sympathize with our weaknesses?

_____

When God came to earth in the person of Jesus Christ, He experienced every temptation we human beings experience. Yet, because He is God, He did not sin. Our God is our Creator. He knows we are weak. He understands our weaknesses, and because He can sympathize with us, we can approach His throne with the assurance that we will find mercy and grace to help us in our time of need. We simply need to humbly approach Him, ask His forgiveness, and bask in His abundant mercy. Our Jesus is our high priest forever. So, let's hold firmly to the faith we have and the assurance that we will receive grace in our time of need.

To close out our week, take a moment to approach His throne of grace. Have you been carrying a burden of guilt or shame? Lay it before Him. He is your high priest forever. He sympathizes with the difficulties you experience in this life. He understands the temptations you face. He loves you, and He always lives to intercede for you (Hebrews 7:25).

> Have you been carrying a burden of guilt or shame? Lay it before Him. He is your high priest forever.

Week 3

Conflicting Intentions

Blessed Righteousness

Abram believed the LORD, and He credited it to him as righteousness.

GENESIS 15:6

Last week, Abram had finally separated from Lot and settled in Hebron, a town west of the Sea of Salt, in Canaan. Lot chose to settle southeast of that same sea, near the town of Sodom. When he was captured by a group of kings who conquered the city of Sodom, Abram rallied his trained servants and rescued his nephew. Abram's mission was successful, and the king of the wicked city of Sodom met him as he returned home. However, when offered Sodom's valuables, Abram made it clear he had not been fighting for Sodom. His sole intention was to rescue his nephew. Abram bluntly refused to accept even a single item from Sodom's treasures.

Melchizedek, priest of God Most High, also met with Abram. This time, it was Abram who was offering a portion of the treasures. He acknowledged his dependence upon and his gratitude toward the Lord as Abram gave God's priest Melchizedek a tenth of all the goods recovered in battle.

We don't know how much time had passed, but sometime after Abram's encounter with these two very different men, Abram was visited by God Himself in the form of a vision.

Let's see what God had to say to His world traveller. Please read Genesis 15:1.

What does God encourage Abram not to do? _____

What two assurances does God give Abram to encourage him and calm his fears?

1) _____ 2) _____

Abram had just witnessed a brutal battle. He and his trained men had won the fight, but people rarely experience the ugliness of war without some lasting effects. After settling back into routine, Abram appears to have been wrestling with some fear, questioning his purpose, and, perhaps, even wondering about the certainty of God's promised son.

In essence, God said, "I am your protector and your defender, Abram." Whatever doubts or fears Abram wrestled with that day, God made it clear that He would shield his servant from future threats like King Kedorlaomer who had dominated the region for all those years. It appears Abram needed to be reassured that he would not be left on his own if he encountered future battles against the people of Canaan.

Have you ever been through a season where you had to defend your principles or protect a loved one on a daily basis? Have you ever laid your head down on your pillow at night, exhausted because you spent the day running through scenarios to overcome a challenge you were experiencing? Have you ever feared the future? Maybe you have never had to physically fight with weapons, but I would guess you have, at times, been confronted with your own vulnerability or felt overwhelmed by fear or anxiety. If so, share the circumstances and note what reassurances you longed to have from God at that time.

> Have you ever been through a season where you had to defend your principles or protect a loved one on a daily basis?

_____

_____

_____

I am guessing Abram had similar needs as the "word of the Lord came to him" in that vision. It appears Abram also might have been wondering if this move to Canaan and his separation from family was all worth it. God made it clear He was not just Abram's protector and defender, but He would also bless Abram (reveal His goodness and kindness) by rewarding His follower's obedience.

Continue reading Genesis 15:2-3 and summarize Abram's response in your own words:

_____

_____

_____

In Abram's mind, there was not any reward God could give him that would compare with having a son. Abram wanted an heir. He wanted a child to call his own. Otherwise, this land of Canaan, his wealth, every possession he owned would be handed down to a mere servant in his household. Abram could not think of any reward that would have meaning in that context.

> In Abram's mind, there was not any reward God could give him that would compare with having a son.

Now, I find God's response incredibly touching. Read Genesis 15:4-5.

Look back at Genesis 12:7. To whom did God say He would give the land?

_____

God never said a servant would be Abram's heir. In today's terms, God was saying this heir would have Abram's genes. His DNA. The heir would be a flesh-and-blood Abram-ite.

Verse 5 says God "took" Abram outside. According to Strong's Exhaustive Concordance, this does not mean God gently took Abram by the hand and led him outside. Instead, this word can be translated "to pluck out, to bring forth or to fetch out" (Strongs 3318). God basically took hold of Abram's arms and moved him outside with, perhaps, a little bit of oomph behind the action. Then, with a strong tone of authority, said to Abram, "look up at the sky and count the stars—if indeed you can count them. So shall your offspring be."

From the Ferguson home, located in the greater Houston, Texas, area, lights from businesses make it difficult to see more than a few stars shining in the night sky. However, our favorite family vacation spot is in the Texas Hill Country, away from all of the hustle and bustle of the city. On clear nights, we sit outside and marvel at the multitude of shining stars and the sheer vastness of the dark sky. Looking up at the stars in that setting is humbling and reminds me to keep my life and my problems in perspective. God, who created our vast universe and knows the source of every star, is far greater than my challenges and powerful enough to accomplish His every purpose.

> Looking up at the stars is humbling and reminds me to keep my life and my problems in perspective.

I imagine Abram had similar thoughts as he indeed looked up at the twinkling blanket of countless stars in the sky that night. He probably felt completely overwhelmed as God said the words, "So shall your offspring be." These offspring would not be the children of Abram's servant, but Abram's own heirs.

Read Genesis 15:6.

When the Creator of the universe promised Abram countless descendants, despite the fact he and Sarai were both old and beyond child-bearing years, Abram chose to believe God.

> When the Creator of the universe promised Abram countless descendants, despite the fact he and Sarai were both old and beyond child-bearing years, Abram chose to believe God.

What did God credit to Abram because of his belief? _____

Righteousness is a forensic term. The definition of forensic is, "pertaining to, connected with, or used in courts of law or public discussion or debate."[14] So righteousness is a term related to the ruling of a judge, in this case, God—the ultimate Judge of all mankind. In this passage, we are being told that God made the ruling that Abram was innocent (righteous) because of his faith. Abram compromised obedience when he settled in Haran and took his family along with him when he left Ur. Abram lied to Pharaoh when he was in Egypt. Yet, because Abram chose to believe God when his life's circumstances showed no evidence that God's promise would come to pass, God declared Abram righteous—innocent of all charges.

> Righteousness is a term related to the ruling of a judge, in this case, God—the ultimate Judge of all mankind.

Read Genesis 15:6 from The Message below:

> *And he believed! Believed God!*
> *God declared him "Set-Right-with-God."*

Now that is an example of God's goodness and kindness if I have ever heard one. Abram believed God, and he received the blessing of righteousness.

WEEK THREE | DAY TWO

An Unprecedented Covenant

When the sun had set and darkness had fallen, a smoking firepot
with a blazing torch appeared and passed between the pieces.

GENESIS 15:17

Our future Patriarch had been encouraged by the Lord; he was assured of God's protection and reminded that the presence of God Himself would be Abram's greatest reward. When Abram chose to believe that his descendants would be as numerous as the stars in the sky, God, as the ultimate Judge of all creation, made the ruling that Abram was righteous—innocent, blameless, and set right with God. Abram obviously was not perfect. His choices were not faultless. However, God, by an abundant act of grace, gave Abram the blessed gift of righteousness because of his faith.

Interestingly, that is not all God had to say to His discouraged follower that day. Please read Genesis 15:7-11.

What question does Abram ask God in verse 8?

_____

Did you notice God did not scold Abram for his doubt? That in itself is an act of mercy and grace on the part of our Sovereign Lord. What animals did God instruct Abram to bring him?

_____   _____   _____

_____   and   _____

The text does not tell us how long it took Abram to select the specific animals from among his herds, but I have to wonder how he would have kept track of their ages. Abram was wealthy in livestock (Genesis 13:2). He had a lot of heifers, goats, and rams from which to choose. His herdsmen didn't have paper and pencils in order to keep logs of birthdates. It is possible they branded the animals with distinguishing marks. We are not told, but whatever the method, Abram took the time to carefully select the requested animals and then brought all of them back before the Lord. What did Abram do to the animals (vs. 10)?

This act of cutting animals in two and arranging the halves opposite each other to create a path between them, was a customary part of "cutting" a covenant. A covenant is a serious, binding agreement between, at least, two parties. Typically, when a covenant like this was made, the terms of the treaty would be agreed upon and then both parties would walk between the slaughtered animals, agreeing that they, too, would be cut into pieces if they broke the agreement.

In the days of the prophet Jeremiah, King Zedekiah made a covenant with the people of Jerusalem. In this agreement, the people vowed to free their slaves, but afterward, changed their minds. They did not keep the terms of the covenant. Read Jeremiah 34:17-20 and note the punishment God said would befall those who broke the covenant:

Abram was obviously familiar with the making of a covenant. He did not have to ask God what to do with the animals. He immediately cut them in half, anticipating the same fate for himself if he failed to adhere to whatever commitment he was about to make. I imagine Abram sat pensively waiting for God to declare the terms of their covenant.

At sunset, the tension at the bloody scene was eclipsed by a "dreadful darkness," and Abram fell into a deep sleep. Please read Genesis 15:12-16.

What did God say Abram could "know for certain"?

According to verse 14, what would happen after the four hundred years of enslavement and mistreatment?

What did God say would happen to Abram? _____

In verses 7-8, God confirmed that He is the same God who spoke to Abram back in Ur and once again promised Abram the land. However, according to verse 16, who did God say would actually gain possession of the land?

_____

On the lines below, summarize the agreement (terms of the covenant) God made with Abram:

_____

_____

_____

I would venture to say, discovering that his descendants would be enslaved and mistreated for four hundred years before they would take possession of the Promised Land, was not exactly the news Abram anticipated. To add to the surprises, Abram would not actually be the one who would take possession of the land, but it would be the fourth generation of Abram-ites. In other words, his great grandchildren's children. Did you notice something missing in the terms of this covenant? Look back through verses 12-16. What did God require Abram to do as part of the terms of this agreement?

_____

Abram, still in a deep sleep, must have been puzzled. Let's see what happened next. Please read Genesis 15:17-20. Who (or what?) passed through the animal carcasses?

_____

Abram was not obligated to do anything in this divinely sealed covenant. Only the smoking firepot and the flaming torch (representing God) passed through the bloody carcasses Abram had arranged on the ground. This firepot probably was not a rounded firepot, like we might picture in an old, rustic cabin. The smoking firepot Abram saw was probably more of "a cylindrical fire-pot, such as is used in the dwelling-houses of the East."[15] Interestingly, many years later, after rescuing His people from the predicted four hundred

EYEWITNESS TO PROMISE: ABRAHAM

years of slavery in Egypt, God manifested His presence in similar fashion to Abram's descendants. Look at Exodus 13:21. How is God's presence revealed in this passage?

The Lord made a one-sided covenant with Abram. He promised to give the land of Canaan to Abram's descendants, and as the firepot, surrounded by a pillar of billowy smoke, and the flaming torch passed through the pieces of dead animals, God confirmed that should the aforementioned events fail to happen, the same fate that befell the slaughtered animals would happen to the Lord. This was a promise of which Abram could be certain. There was nothing Abram or his descendants had to do in order for this promise to come to pass. God alone took the responsibility for its fulfillment.

> The Lord made a one-sided covenant with Abram.

Read Acts 7:2-7 and note what God said Abram's (Abraham) descendants would do when they returned and took possession of the land:

The text does not say, but I would imagine Abram did some worshipping himself after he awoke from that deep sleep there in Canaan, still overwhelmed by the gracious terms of God's unprecedented, one-sided covenant.

WEEK THREE | DAY THREE

An Alternative Offspring

*". . . so she said to Abram, "The LORD has kept me from having children.
Go, sleep with my slave; perhaps I can build a family through her."*

GENESIS 16:2

As we open our Bibles to a new chapter of Scripture today, many years have passed since Abram's covenantal encounter with God. Now in his mid-eighties, he and his wife, Sarai, were still waiting on the child God had promised. One day, Sarai looked at one of her household slaves, a woman named Hagar, and came up with what she believed would be a great solution to the couple's childless dilemma.

Read Genesis 16:1-2.

What was Sarai's idea? _____

Look carefully at verse 2. Who did Sarai say would build this long-awaited family?

> One day, Sarai looked at one of her household slaves, a woman named Hagar, and came up with what she believed would be a great solution to the couple's childless dilemma.

Sarai was tired of waiting. She was probably frustrated and, perhaps, a little bitter because the Lord had not given her any children. Sarai decided it was time to get her family started. She was determined to make *her* dream of having a child into a reality, *her* way.

When it seems like God is taking too long to act, sometimes the self-focused "I" in us will conjure up a plan to help Him out. Have you ever felt discouraged or bitter, maybe even a little angry at God, and begun to manipulate people or circumstances in an attempt to get your desired result? If so, what were some of the emotions that prompted you to take control? If not, what emotions do you believe Sarai was feeling when she came up with her plan?

_____

_____

Let's see how Sarai's plan unfolded. Read Genesis 16:3-5.

What happened once Hagar discovered she was pregnant?

_____

Whom did Sarai blame for "the wrong" she was suffering?

_____

> Have you ever felt discouraged or bitter, maybe even a little angry at God, and begun to manipulate people or circumstances in an attempt to get your desired result?

"In the legal custom of that day, a barren woman could give her maid to her husband as a wife, and the child born of that union was regarded as the first wife's child."[16] Sarai's proposition was perfectly legal and probably seemed logical. But once again, Abram relied upon human reasoning, rather than seeking God, before coming up with a solution to what he and Sarai perceived to be a problem. Read Proverbs 3:5-6 below from The Message and circle what Abram appears to have had a natural tendency to do when faced with uncertainty. Then underline what he should have done.

> *Trust God from the bottom of your heart; don't try to figure out everything on your own. Listen for God's voice in everything you do, everywhere you go; He's the One who will keep you on track* (MSG).

Abram agreed to Sarai's plan even though deep down in the depths of his being, he had to realize sleeping with a servant was not the means by which God intended to fulfill His promise. Whatever thoughts rationalized Abram's actions, he once again failed to seek God's counsel. He failed to "listen for God's voice" before he consummated Sarai's plan. As often happens when we try to make God's plans come to pass our way, Abram and Sarai's circumstances became more complicated. Once Hagar became pregnant, she began to despise Sarai. After all, she knew

> As often happens when we try to make God's plans come to pass our way, Abram and Sarai's circumstances became more complicated.

the moment her child was born, Sarai intended to take him as her own. To make matters worse, every time Sarai saw Hagar's enlarged belly, she was probably reminded of her inability to give her husband the one thing he wanted more than anything else—a child. To further complicate the situation, I imagine the idea of Abram sleeping with Hagar stirred up some jealousy within Sarai's discouraged heart.

Imagine yourself in each woman's position. Note the emotions you might feel that would fuel discord between you.

Sarai: _____

_____

Hagar: _____

_____

As Abram prepared for the birth of his first child, he must have been excited. However, the backdrop of that excitement certainly had to be a sense of regret because he was not sharing this moment with Sarai. Having a child had been their dream for many, many years.

Read Genesis 16:5-6. What was Abram's solution to the conflict between Sarai and Hagar?

_____

Abram took a passive approach to the situation. In his defense, this whole plan had been Sarai's idea. Yet, when the reality was far more difficult to deal with than she ever anticipated, Sarai's anger was directed toward her husband. Abram was in what we might call a no-win situation. Rather than upsetting either woman, this man-with-two-wives opted to let Sarai decide how to handle Hagar. According to verse 6, what did Sarai do, and how did Hagar respond?

_____

What a mess. Sarai was angry, Abram was disengaged, and the mistreated and frightened mother of the child Abram and Sarai thought they so desperately wanted was out by herself in the desert. Once again, God had not been consulted, but He was keenly aware of the mess His future Patriarch had created as he awaited the arrival of the promised son. Please read Genesis 16:7-15.

Shur was located near the eastern border of Egypt (1 Samuel 15:7). Hagar fled toward her former home and stopped at a spring along the way for a drink and some rest. She was alone. She had been used by Abram, mistreated by Sarai, and the precious child she was carrying was going to be snatched away from her the moment he breathed his first breath. Hagar was desperate and probably felt like no one was aware of the pain and mistreatment she had endured. But our Lord saw the way Sarai mistreated Hagar. He was aware of Abram's passivity and understood Hagar's fears. According to verse 7, who met Hagar at that spring in the desert?

This is the first time Scripture talks about "the angel of the Lord." We don't know much about this visitor, but according to The Bible Knowledge Commentary, this may have been the first recorded appearance of the pre-incarnate Christ.[17] When Hagar told him she was running away, what was she told to do?

That probably was not the answer Hagar wanted to hear. She wanted to go back home to Egypt. She wanted to be free of her obligations to her mistress. She probably wanted to keep her son. However, what seemed to matter most to Hagar was knowing that God heard and saw all that she had endured. What name did God give her son, and what was the reason for that particular name (vs. 11)?

> What seemed to matter most to Hagar was knowing that God heard and saw all that she had endured.

By what name did Hagar call the Lord (vs.13)?

Ishmael means "God hears." Indeed, He had heard it all. He had seen it all. Our God sees and hears and knows all about the matters that concern His people. This alternative child Hagar bore to Abram was a reminder to everyone involved that God was aware of all that had happened. As we will see in our studies next week, Ishmael would indeed live in hostility toward the promised child, yet to be born to Abram and his first wife, Sarai. In fact, the descendants of this alternative child of Abram's (Arabs) still live in hostility toward the descendants of the promised child (Jews) to this day. Ishmael was an alternative offspring who ushered in endless consequences.

Father of a Multitude

"No longer will you be called Abram; your name will be Abraham,
for I have made you a father of many nations."

GENESIS 17:5

O ur last lesson ended with the birth of Ishmael when Abram was eighty-six years old. He and Sarai had attempted to help God along and make God's plan come to pass their way. As a result, the relationships in their household had become strained and complicated.

Look at Genesis 17:1. How old was Abram as we begin this new chapter?

Considering the dynamics in Abram's tents, I would say the thirteen years between these chapters were stressful, long years for the Patriarch. In Day Three's lesson, God told Hagar to return and submit to Sarai, which she did. However, Scripture is silent about the then-current state of the relationships within Abram's household, which now included a teenaged Ishmael.

To refresh your memory, look back at Genesis 16:12. What did God tell Hagar about her son, Ishmael?

I am guessing Ishmael's presence served as a catalyst for conflicts within this blended family. As chapter 17 begins, I think it is safe to assume ninety-nine-year-old Abram was thankful for an heir. He had always wanted a son. He was probably a family man and had done his best to raise his "wild donkey" of a boy well. However, I would also guess Abram's alternative offspring had often created a tent-ful of challenges.

How does God introduce Himself to Abram in Genesis 17:1?

In Hebrew, this name for God is *El-Shaddai*, and it is the first time God introduces Himself by this name in Scripture.[18] The name emphasizes God's power and sufficiency, His ability to accomplish His divine purposes. In essence, God was making it clear He did not need Abram and Sarai's creative family planning in order to bring them the child He had promised. The impatient couple had attempted to help God with His plan, and, by this time in the story, Abram had been dealing with the consequences of his actions for over thirteen years. Did he love Ishmael? Certainly he did. Did God have plans for Ishmael? He made it clear to Hagar that He did (Genesis 16:11-12).

> God was making it clear He did not need Abram and Sarai's creative family planning in order to bring them the child He had promised.

Abram had been presumptuous, perhaps even reckless as he waited for God to produce the child He promised. Yet, despite all of his mistakes, God did not abandon Abram, and He still intended to keep His promises.

What do the following verses tell you about God's faithfulness to keep his promises?

Numbers 23:19 _____

Psalm 145:13 _____

God does not lie and He does not change His mind. He is worthy of our trust. Our God is *El Shaddai*, a powerful, all-sufficient God who is faithful in all He does and is able to keep His promises.

Read Genesis 17:1-2. What instruction did God give Abram in verse 1?

Abram believed God would grant him a child, and that faith had been credited to him as righteousness (Genesis 15:6). But as Abram waited for the fulfillment of that promise, he became impatient. His devoted heart was tested on the crucible of a long, uncertain waiting period. Although Abram had moments of strong faith in God, his test had revealed some doubt and self-reliance. Rather than continuing to talk to God and seek His plan for the waiting period, Abram relied upon human logic and cultural customs to determine the right next step along his faith journey.

God told Abram to "walk faithfully" before Him. Young's Literal Translation reads, "walk habitually before me." In other words, God said, "Abram, seek Me consistently."

What weaknesses have your recent tests or trials revealed? How consistent are you at seeking God's counsel along your faith journey? Have you ever had to wait for a long time for some adverse circumstances to change? If so, what actions did you take that might have prompted God to say to you, "Beloved, seek Me consistently"?

_____

_____

_____

Abram and Sarai had taken control and tried to force God's will to happen their way. However, in order to live out God's call for his life, Abram needed to habitually seek his all-sufficient, all-powerful God and consistently trust Him to keep His promises. When Abram had asked God how he could know his descendants would possess the Promised Land, God made a one-sided covenant with Abram, guaranteeing His promises would come to pass. His descendants would be as numerous as the stars in the sky, and, without a doubt, they would one day possess the land.

According to Genesis 17:3, how did Abram react to God's words?

> God told Abram to "walk faithfully" before Him. God made a one-sided covenant with Abram, guaranteeing His promises would come to pass.

_____

Abram fell on his face in surrender. He was ready to do this God's way. He was ready to follow God's plan. He was ready to trust in his all-sufficient, all-powerful God.

Let's see what God said next. Please read Genesis 17:3-5.

What did God promise Abram in verse 4? _____

What name did God give Abram, and what was the reason for the change?

_____

God changed Abram's name to Abraham, which "is a dialectical variant of the name Abram. Its significance is in the wordplay with the Hebrew word *av-hamon*, which means "the father of a multitude."[19] The wait and the challenges Abram had experienced had prepared him. Abram (Exalted Father) was now ready to become Abraham (Father of a Multitude). He was now ready to be the father of many nations.

> Abraham was now ready to be the father of many nations.

Look closely at verse 5. Who was it that made Abraham a father of many nations?

Abram and Sarai may have tried to make God's plans come to pass their way, but at the right time, the Lord Himself would make good on His promise. The changing of Abram's name to Abraham signified the beginning of a new season in Abraham's journey with God. Let's see what else God had to say to His newly named Father of a Multitude.

Read Genesis 17:6-8 below. Then circle each of the specific promises related to His covenant with Abraham:

> *I will make you very fruitful; I will make nations of you, and kings will come from you. I will establish my covenant as an everlasting covenant between me and you and your descendants after you for the generations to come, to be your God and the God of your descendants after you. The whole land of Canaan, where you now reside as a foreigner, I will give as an everlasting possession to you and your descendants after you; and I will be their God* (NIV).

As Abraham listened to all God promised to one day do for his descendants, he must have been overwhelmed by the goodness and kindness of his God. Before the appointed patriarch ever left Ur, he had been promised his name would be great (Genesis 12:2). I can think of no more glorious name for the one who lived the majority of his life as a fatherless Exalted Father than to be deemed in both name and station Father of a Multitude.

WEEK THREE | **DAY FIVE**

Personal Application

Application from Day One

To refresh your memory, re-read Genesis 15: 1-6.

Although there was no tangible evidence in Abram's life circumstances to substantiate God's promise of descendants as numerous as stars in the sky, Abram chose to believe God would somehow make this promise come to pass. That belief was credited to Abram as righteousness.

Read Romans 4:1-5 and summarize the passages in your own words:

_____

_____

Now read Romans 3:21-24 and note what is credited to all who place their faith in Jesus:

_____

As believers in Christ, we are declared righteous—inno-cent of all charges—regardless of the mistakes or failings of our past. As with Abram, it is a gift that we could never have earned.

> As believers in Christ, we are declared righteous—innocent of all charges.

Application from Day Two

In our Day Two lesson, God made a one-sided covenant with Abram. Look again at Genesis 15:4-7. What two promises did God make Abram before He made the covenant with him?

1) _____

2) _____

Now re-read Genesis 15:8-19. Only God (represented by the smoking firepot and blazing torch) passed between the animal pieces as the covenant agreement was sealed. Therefore, in order for these promises to come to pass, what was required of Abram?

God alone was the One who accepted the responsibility for making sure the promises associated with His covenant would, indeed, happen. Later in our study, we will further explore the glorious implications of this one-sided covenant—not just rest in the assurance that God is worthy of our trust.for Abram, but also for you and for me. For now,

Are you in the middle of a waiting period? Have you tried to help God out with your own creative plans? What situation in your life do you need to entrust to our trustworthy God?

> Have you tried to help God out with your own creative plans?

Take a moment to pray and lay that need before our Lord. He does not need your help. He is able and aware of everything you need.

Application from Days Three and Four

Abram and Sarai had attempted to help God's plans come to pass their way, and the servant, Hagar, whom they had used and mistreated in the process, attempted to flee back to her homeland of Egypt. Although she probably felt like no one was aware of all she had been through, the appearance of "the angel of the Lord," near a spring in the desert, confirmed that God heard and saw everything that had taken place.

Read the following passages and note what you learn about God's awareness of the events that take place on earth:

Psalm 33:13-14 _____

Psalm 139:7-12 _____

Hebrews 4:13 _____

Nothing is hidden from God's sight. There is no wrong you have experienced, no manipulation you have endured, no

> Nothing is hidden from God's sight.

pain you have suffered, that has escaped His notice. Everything is laid bare before the eyes of our Lord.

Re-read Genesis 17:1-4. What name did God use for Himself in verse 1, and what does the name mean? (Look back at Day Four's lesson if you need to refresh your memory.)

God was able to make His promises come to pass. He did not need Abram and Sarai's assistance. Abram needed to stop relying upon cultural customs or his own clever solutions to his problems and seek God consistently.

According to verse 3, how did Abram respond to the realization that, despite all of his mistakes, God still intended to keep His promise?

You know, I have been most overwhelmed by the goodness and kindness of our God when He has made me aware of His presence and activity in my life despite the undeniable consequences that have confronted me with my own sin—moments when I was keenly aware that I am completely undeserving of His mercy and love. That realization has, at times, caused me to fall on my face before Him in surrender.

According to Romans 3:23, who is without sin? _____

Sin happens when we do not meet God's expectations or live up to the standards outlined in His Word. The *New International Encyclopedia of Bible Words* indicates there are three Hebrew words our English Bibles translate as sin. The principal word for sin is *hata*, which means "to miss the mark." The word *pesa*, meaning rebellion or transgression, "indicates a revolt against God's standard," and the third word is *awon*, which is "a deviation from or a twisting of God's standard."[20]

As you consider all three definitions for sin, is there any doubt that there is not a living, breathing human being who has not sinned? That, my friend, is without a doubt a rhetorical question.

Roman 6:23 is a good-news, bad-news passage about sin. First, the bad news. What does our sin (any form of it) earn us?

And the good news? _____

If you have accepted Jesus as your Lord and your Savior, your sins are not counted against you. You, just like Abraham, have been declared righteous in the sight of our God. If you have not accepted Jesus as Savior, take a peek at Romans 10:9. What do you have to do in order to be saved?

_____

It is that simple. Will you consider doing that today? All you have to do is accept the free gift of salvation and eternal life Jesus offers you. Will you pray this prayer with me now?

Heavenly Father, I believe that Jesus is Your Son, who came to this earth as a man and died on a cross for my sins. I acknowledge to You that I am a sinner and I need forgiveness. Your Word says in Romans 10:9, "That if [I] confess with [my] mouth, 'Jesus is Lord,' and believe in [my] heart that God raised Him from the dead, [I] will be saved." I do believe, Lord, and I take Jesus today as my Lord and Savior. Thank you, Father, for saving me from my mistakes and my rebellion. In Jesus' name I pray.

If you prayed that prayer for the first time, please talk to your small group leader or pastor. Rejoice in the fact you are not condemned. You, like Abraham, are in right standing with God, free of guilt and shame, through the free gift of salvation through our Jesus.

Week 4

Matters of Preservation

Covenantal Promise

Therefore, the promise comes by faith, so that it may be by grace and may be guaranteed to all Abraham's offspring—not only to those who are of the law but also to those who have the faith of Abraham. He is the father of us all.

ROMANS 4:16

As we closed our Week Three lessons, Abram's name had been changed to Abraham, reflecting God's covenantal promise to make the Patriarch's descendants as numerous as the stars in the sky. The covenant also confirmed God would bless those descendants with what became known as the Promised Land. From this point forward in our study, even when referring back to events that occurred while our protagonist was named Abram, we will continue to use his new, covenantal name, Abraham.

Before we continue with his story, I want to spend our time today solidifying what we have learned about the promises God made to Abraham. Those promises were confirmed with an oath, often referred to as the Abrahamic Covenant. Some of the information we will study today will feel like review, but these covenantal passages are important because they provide a foundation for our understanding of Scripture as a whole. I encourage you to read every verse referenced in today's lesson and ask God to help you look at each of them with fresh eyes, as though you were reading them for the first time. Abraham was an eyewitness to the promise, guaranteed by a covenant, which not only had profound meaning for his blood descendants, but also has great significance for us today.

> Abraham was an eyewitness to the promise, guaranteed by a covenant, which not only had profound meaning for his blood descendants, but also has great significance for us today.

So, let's begin by once again reading Genesis 12:1-3. What word was repeated in various forms throughout verses 2-3 and is a primary focus for these passages? (Look back at the Week One, Day Two lesson, if you need some help.)

What did God say He would make Abraham in verse 2?

Who did God say would be blessed *through* Abraham (vs. 3)?

Now read Genesis 13:14-17. What two promises did God make to Abraham in verses 15 and 16?

Verse 15:_____ Verse 16:_____

Please read Genesis 15:1-6. What further clarification did God make in verse 4 regarding the offspring God promised Abraham?

The word translated in our Bibles as "offspring" in verse 5 is a Hebrew word that means "seed." Let's see what some other passages in our Bibles teach us about the promises God made to Abraham and to his "seed."

Please read Galatians 3:7-9. According to verse 7, who are considered children of Abraham?

According to verse 8, how does the gospel (the good news of salvation by faith in Jesus) relate to the promise in Genesis 12:3?

Abraham's descendants fall into two categories: natural, also called Jews, and spiritual, who are non-Jews (Gentiles) who have placed their faith in Jesus. The Bible Knowledge Commentary explains it this way:

> Any discussion of the seed of Abraham must first take into account his natural seed [his natural descendants] . . . But there is also the spiritual seed of Abraham who are not Jews. These are the Gentiles who believe [in Christ] and become Abraham's spiritual seed.[21]

Now read Galatians 3:15-16. Who is the Seed of Abraham?

WEEK FOUR

Stay with me here! Please read Galatians 3:28-29 and note what you learn about those who have placed their faith in (or belong to) Jesus Christ (Abraham's Seed).

Jesus is the Seed of Abraham, and when you placed your faith in Jesus, by your association with Him, you became Abraham's spiritual seed and an heir to the promise God made to Abraham and to his Seed. You are counted among the people of all nations (Genesis 12:3) God said would be blessed through Abraham. God's covenantal promise was three-fold. Let's look at each aspect of the Abrahamic Covenant:

1). <u>God promised Abraham's descendants land</u> (Genesis 13:15). The land had specific boundaries and Abraham's natural descendants, called Israelites, took possession of much of that territory when Joshua led them into the Promised Land (Joshua 1-24). But they have not yet inhabited all of it. This promise also held significance for Abraham's spiritual descendants.

> Jesus is the Seed of Abraham, and when you placed your faith in Jesus, by your association with Him, you became an heir to the promise God made to Abraham and to his Seed.

Read Hebrews 11:8-10. What was Abraham looking forward to, according to verse 10?

As believers in Christ, we are Abraham's seed (Galatians 3:29) and we can look forward to our eternal Promised Land, in Heaven—a city whose architect and builder is our God.

2). <u>God promised to bless Abraham and his offspring</u> (Genesis 12:2-3). In essence, God promised to express His kindness and goodness to Abraham, as well as his natural and spiritual offspring. The word "kindness" as used in the Old Testament is usually a translation of the Hebrew word *hesed*, which means to act in a loyal, loving way to a person, and it is related to His covenant. "God's love moves Him to be kind to those with whom he has established a covenant relationship."[22] Let's define this aspect of the Abrahamic Covenant as God's promise to express His kindness, *hesed,* toward Abraham as well as his natural and spiritual offspring. He promised to *bless* them.

3). <u>God promised Abraham a seed</u>. It is through this Seed (ultimately Christ) that all nations would be blessed (Genesis 12:3). Let's look at this promise a little more closely. Turn back to Genesis 17:7. With whom did God make this covenant and how long does it last?

_____

Now read Genesis 17:9-14. What did God instruct Abraham and his natural descendants to do as a sign of their covenant relationship with Him?

_____

Interestingly, read Colossians 2:9-15. According to verse 11, who circumcises Abraham's spiritual descendants (believers in Christ)?

_____

I do not want to get graphic, but the Apostle Paul wanted us to understand that when we accepted Jesus as Savior, our flesh nature was taken away, much like skin was taken away during circumcision, and the Spirit's work in our hearts and lives is evidence of the circumcision performed in our hearts. We are new creations. The old nature is gone, and new life in Christ has come (2 Corinthians 5:17). Baptism is an outward expression of what has taken place in our hearts. Denominations differ in their opinions about the purpose and method of baptism. If you have never taken this important step in your relationship with Jesus, or you have questions, I urge you to seek out a leader or pastor in your church. Ask questions. Read more about what the Bible says regarding this topic. Then act upon what you learn.

As a way of closing today's lesson, please read Romans 4:16-18 and note your relationship to Abraham (vs. 16):

_____

This mystery is that through the gospel the Gentiles are heirs together with Israel, members together of one body, and sharers together in the promise in Christ Jesus. (Ephesians 3:6)

WEEK FOUR | DAY TWO

Noteworthy Names

Then God said, "Yes, but your wife Sarah will bear you a son, and you will call him Isaac.

GENESIS 17:19

In yesterday's lesson, Abraham was commanded to circumcise his descendants. Circumcision was an act of obedience that reflected what had already taken place in a man's heart. In Deuteronomy 10:16, Israel's great leader Moses told the people, "Circumcise your hearts, therefore, and do not be stiff-necked any longer." Later in Deuteronomy, Moses said, "The Lord your God will circumcise your hearts and the hearts of your descendants, so that you may love Him with all your heart and with all your soul, and live" (Deuteronomy 30:6). Circumcision served as a sign of one's covenant relationship with and devotion to the Lord.

Let's see what else God had to say to Abraham that day. Please read Genesis 17:15-16.

What name was given to Sarai? _____

In Hebrew, Sarah means Princess.[23] Once again, God made a slight change in a name to symbolize a new beginning in this journey of faith. The Father of a Multitude and his Princess would bear a child whose descendants would produce kings of peoples. The past was left behind, and the couple were to move forward with new names, signifying the promises of their God.

Read Genesis 17:17 and note how Abraham responded to this awe inspiring news:

_____

I picture Abraham falling face down in awe of all God had just declared, and then laughing to himself as he considered the oddity of a ninety-year old woman and a hundred-year old man having a child. He was not disputing God's statement. He was simply expressing delight and embracing the utter peculiarity of God's method for producing the promised son.

Read Psalm 126:1-3. What did the people do in response to the great things the Lord had done for them?

_____

Laughter is often a sign of joy. But I believe God appreciates and ordains a healthy sense of humor, and Abraham's laughter was appropriate, considering the situation. However, as he reflected upon the reality that his firstborn, Ishmael, would not be the heir to God's promise, Abraham's countenance became a little more somber.

> I believe God appreciates and ordains a healthy sense of humor, and Abraham's laughter was appropriate, considering the situation.

Please read Genesis 17:18-22.

What did God tell Abraham to name the son Sarah would bear?

The son whose promised birth caused his daddy to laugh with delight would be named Isaac, which means "he laughs."[24] I think God enjoyed His relationship with the Patriarch.

> Has it ever occurred to you that God enjoys His relationship with you?

Has it ever occurred to you that God enjoys His relationship with you, too? What do the following passages suggest about the way God feels toward those with whom He has a relationship?

Psalm 147:11 _____

Psalm 149:1-5 _____

Zephaniah 3:17 _____

Take a moment to talk to the One who delights in you. Write a prayer below, sharing whatever you have on your heart at this time.

_____

_____

_____

Look again at Genesis 17:19-22. What did God promise to do for each of Abraham's sons?

Ishmael: _____

Isaac: _____

WEEK FOUR

I imagine the most important part of God's message regarding Ishmael was when He said, "I have heard you." As parents, when we cry out to our God on behalf of our children, we do not always know what is best for them. We sometimes struggle to know what specifics to pray. But we want assurance that God will keep them under His watchful eye. We want to know He has heard our pleas and will move on their behalf. God heard Abraham and understood the ache of the Patriarch's fatherly heart. God would bring good things to Ishmael's life, but that son was never intended to be the one through whom He would fulfill His promise.

> As parents, when we cry out to our God on behalf of our children, we do not always know what is best for them. We sometimes struggle to know what specifics to pray.

Now read Genesis 17:23-27.

What did Abraham do once he accepted God's plan for each of his sons?

_____

Abraham obeyed. He might have had a heavy heart as he circumcised Ishmael, but he resolved himself to God's plan and carefully did everything he was commanded to do. As the next chapter begins, Abraham is sitting at the entrance of his tent near those great trees of Mamre. This is the first time so far in our study that we are told Abraham was sitting. This man who was constantly on the move was found resting at the entrance to his tent in the heat of the day. Let's see what happened as Abraham rested at the entrance to his tent.

Please read Genesis 18:1-8.

We do not know much about these mysterious men, but somehow one of the three traveling companions represented the presence of the Lord. In verse 3, how did Abraham address the men, and what was his request?

Although the NIV does not reflect it, the word "Lord" in Abraham's greeting was the Hebrew word *Adonay*, and this word is only used as a proper name for God (*Strong's*). In other words, Abraham was asking God to eat with him and spend time with him under that tree at the entrance to his tent. When his invitation was accepted, Abraham sprang into action. He hurried into the tent and told Sarah to bake some bread, and then "he ran" and selected what we can only assume was a choice calf. Even Abraham's servant hurried to prepare the meal.

According to verse 8, what posture did Abraham take as his mysterious guests ate?

The man Abraham addressed as *Adonay* was probably, once again, an appearance of the pre-incarnate Christ. Look ahead for a moment. Genesis 19:1 refers to these two additional men who visited Abraham. How are they described?

Abraham was probably hosting the Lord and two of His angels there near the tree of Mamre. Having some sense of the indescribable privilege of that moment, Abraham offered his best and stood attentively near as they ate.

Please read Genesis 18:9-15.

How did Sarah respond as the arrival of the promised son was discussed among the men?

> The difference in God's response to the laughter of Abraham and Sarah serves as a reminder that the Lord knows the thoughts and motivations behind our words, and our laughter.

Obviously, Sarah's laughter was motivated not by delight at the oddity of such an event but by a lack of faith, perhaps expressed with a hint of sarcasm. The profound difference in God's response to the laughter of Abraham and Sarah serves as a stark reminder that the Lord knows the thoughts and motivations behind our words, and our laughter. The couple would indeed have a son in their old age, and both Abraham's happiness and Sarah's cynicism were divinely memorialized in the noteworthy name of their soon-to-be born child of the promise: Isaac.

WEEK FOUR | DAY THREE

Persistent Intercession

Then he said, "May the Lord not be angry,
but let me speak just once more. What if only ten can be found there?"
He answered, "For the sake of ten, I will not destroy it."

GENESIS 18:32

When we last saw Abraham, he was hosting three men, probably comprised of the pre-incarnate Christ and two angels. The timing of the Lord's promise to provide a child was clarified when Abraham was told Sarah would have that son "about this time next year." But in addition to confirming the arrival of Abraham's Child of Promise, there was another purpose for the mysterious men's visit.

Please read Genesis 18:16-21.

What cities were the topic of discussion as Abraham "walked along with [the men] to see them on their way"?

_____ and _____

Read the following passages and note what you learn about these cities.

Isaiah 3:9 _____

Ezekiel 16:49-50 _____

Jude 1:7 _____

According to Genesis 18:21, what did the Lord say He was going to do because of the outcry against Sodom and Gomorrah?

As we have discussed before, God is omniscient. He already knew the gravity of the sins taking place in the cities. If you are familiar with the history of these cities, you know God destroyed them because of the depth of the sin of the people there. We can only assume Abraham was told of God's investigation so that when those cities were destroyed, the Patriarch would be aware of the depravity of the people living there and recognize that God's punishment is never dispensed unjustly.

Let's see how Abraham responded to the realization that God planned to destroy the city in which his nephew was living.

Please read Genesis 18:22-26.

Abraham was obviously distressed. He asked the question in verse 25, "Will not the judge of all the earth do right?" How did God respond to Abraham's plea?

Interestingly, there was another town mentioned later in Scripture that deserved an outpouring of God's wrath. That town was named Nineveh. However, before destroying the town, as God planned to do to Sodom and Gomorrah, the Lord sent a prophet named Jonah to warn the people and encourage them to turn from their wickedness. Although Jonah ran from the Lord's mission (and spent a few days sulking in the belly of a fish before he was ready to obey), Jonah did eventually go to Nineveh and proclaim to the people, "Forty more days and Nineveh will be overthrown" (Jonah 3:4). Amazingly, the people believed God's warning through Jonah and they were spared. However, rather than rejoicing over the people who had been saved, Jonah was angry with God because he believed Nineveh deserved God's wrath.

How is God described in Jonah 4:1-2?

We do not know if God sent prior warnings to Sodom and Gomorrah. But we do know God relents from sending calamity. If fifty righteous people had lived in Sodom, God would have spared the whole place for their sake (Genesis 18:26).

However, Abraham seemed to have a sense there were not fifty righteous people in Sodom. Our passionate protagonist continued to intercede on behalf of the town. Let's see what additional requests Abraham made of the Lord. Please read Genesis 18:27-33.

> If fifty righteous people had lived in Sodom, God would have spared the whole place for their sake (Genesis 18:26).

Abraham was not disrespectful, but he was persistent in his heartfelt prayers for that city. As the Patriarch returned home, what assurance did he have from the Lord?

Meanwhile, the two angels arrived in Sodom. Please read Genesis 19:1-3.

Look back at Genesis 18:1-5. What similarities do you find between Abraham's greeting of the men and Lot's greeting?

What did each man serve these mysterious guests?

Abraham: _____

Lot: _____

Lot was hospitable toward the men, just as Abraham had been. However, the similarities between the visits end there. Abraham recognized the men represented the presence of the Lord Himself and prepared an extraordinary banquet for these honored guests. Lot extended a common greeting "My lords" and provided a common meal. No choice calf. No curds and milk. Lot did not seem to have any sense that these two men were actually angels of the Lord.

Before the angels could even settle in for the evening, the depravity of Lot's community became abundantly clear. Please read Genesis 19:4-8.

What demand did the men from every part of Sodom make of Lot, and what alternative did he offer?

Lot offering up his daughters as an alternative to the men raping his guests is a detail that is difficult for this mother-of-a-daughter to fathom. I must say, every daughter should find protection under the roof of her father. Sadly, in addition to Lot residing in the wicked city of Sodom, it appears the wickedness of Sodom had begun to take up residency within the heart of Lot.

Let's see how this troubling scene at Lot's house ended. Please read Genesis 19:9-22.

According to verse 13, what were the angels sent to do to the cities of Sodom and Gomorrah?

_____

Look back at God's agreement with Abraham in Genesis 18:32. What conclusion can you draw about the cities?

_____

For our final reading today, what does 2 Peter 2:7-8 tell you about Lot?

_____

Lot's behavior that day in Sodom did not reflect the behavior of a righteous man. Yet, only God knew the torment Lot experienced as a result of the "depraved conduct" that surrounded him on a daily basis. I do not have a neat and tidy way of explaining the description of Lot as "that righteous man." Perhaps Lot was deeply influenced by his uncle but had also been corrupted by his environment. Maybe God simply rescued Lot because Abraham had his nephew in mind as he prayed for the righteous people in Sodom. Maybe Lot's actions did not reflect what he knew in his heart to be right. Scripture does not make it clear. However, there are two principles that do become clear from this event. God takes sin seriously and it is only because of His mercy and grace that any of us are saved.

> God takes sin seriously and it is only because of His mercy and grace that any of us are saved.

For the wages of sin is death, but the gift of God is eternal life in Christ Jesus our Lord (Romans 6:23).

WEEK FOUR | DAY FOUR

A Merciful Deliverance

When he hesitated, the men grasped his hand and the hands of his wife
and of his two daughters and led them safely out of the city,
for the Lord was merciful to them.

GENESIS 19:16

As we finished our Day Three lesson, Lot and his family were fleeing Sodom and seeking safety in the small neighboring city of Zoar. God had been merciful to Lot and his family (Genesis 19:16) and delivered them from the impending destruction of the wicked city, probably because of the prayers of God's friend Abraham.

Look again at Genesis 19:16. How did Lot initially respond to the angels' instructions to leave Sodom?

_____

Rather than grabbing his family members by the hand and heading immediately for the hills, Lot hesitated. At first reading, this seems like an odd response. But I would venture to say most of us have hesitated or tried to cling to the familiar when we became aware that the life with which we had become comfortable was about to change.

Have you ever found yourself clinging to the familiar or delaying a move when faced with a major change in your surroundings or circumstances? If so, what pervaded your thoughts and how does that experience help you understand why Lot might have hesitated to leave Sodom?

_____

_____

Please re-read Genesis 19:17-22.

Lot not only hesitated, he negotiated with the angels, despite the warnings of the destruction that would soon befall Sodom. In that moment of chaos and stress, Lot appears to have been overcome with fear and uncertainty. He did not believe he could get to the mountains in time, so rather than trusting God to get his family there safely, he asked for a compromise and the angels graciously granted his request.

According to verse 17, what instructions had the angels given Lot and his family as they left?

Let's see what happened as they fled. Please read Genesis 19:23-26.

What did God bring raining down on the wicked cities of Sodom and Gomorrah?

The story of the destruction of Sodom and Gomorrah is one of the most widely known stories in the Bible. Yet, it is still difficult for us to read as we imagine all of the people that perished there. Lot and his family were spared, but as the burning sulfur began to rain down on the cities, I would guess grief began to well up in their displaced hearts.

What did Lot's wife do and what happened as a result?

Mrs. Lot knew she could never return to the home she had probably cleaned every day for years. She knew the reason for the destruction, and over the years there, she probably complained often about the influence that depraved city had on her children. She may have expected life to be far less challenging for her family in a new town without the pervasive corruption. However, even positive change can cause us to pause and ponder and hold on to places where we have settled and made memories, even when we recognize the struggles and challenges we are leaving behind.

I remember when my aunt was in the hospital, in the final stages of her battle with terminal cancer. She was a believer in Christ and knew being in the presence of Jesus would be so much better than remaining here on earth. However,

> Even positive change can cause us to pause and ponder and hold on to places where we have settled and made memories, even when we recognize the struggles and challenges we are leaving behind.

despite the severity of her pain, she kept asking God to allow her to linger just a little longer. She wanted to feel her husband's touch and see her son's face a few more times. She wanted to have just a few more conversations with family members. She wanted to soak up her surroundings and hold on to the life she had known and loved.

Mrs. Lot may have been fleeing with her feet, but her heart lingered in Sodom. She "looked back" and sadly, her desire to remain in the past caused her to be preserved there permanently as a pillar of salt. Some believe this description of Lot's wife is simply a metaphoric warning not to cherish and hold tightly to sin. But the first century historian Josephus said of the pillar, "I have seen it, and it remains at this day."[25] I personally believe Lot's wife was indeed turned into a pillar of salt and, as such, serves as a metaphoric warning not to cling to the past or cherish past sins.

How are Sodom and Gomorrah described in Zephaniah 2:9?

WEEK FOUR

Are there any past sins you think of fondly? Do you sometimes long to return to the past? Be careful. Avoid the weeds and salt pits of your past. Sometimes those cherished sins of yesteryear can be preserved in our hearts, making us more susceptible to revisiting them in the future. Let's ask God to make old patterns of sin eternal wastelands to which we never return. Resist the urge to look back longingly. Lifestyles of sin are just as deadly to our spiritual wellness today as they were to the residents of Sodom and Gomorrah in Lot's day.

> Do you sometimes long to return to the past?

Now read Genesis 19:27-29. According to verse 29, why was Lot spared?

What does James 5:15-16 tell you happens as a result of the prayers of a righteous person?

Please read Romans 4:18-24. What is credited to us through our belief in the One who raised Jesus our Lord from the dead?

Abraham's faith was credited to him as righteousness (Genesis 15:6), and the same is true of us today. Our prayers are just as powerful and effective as the prayers of Abraham. As we close this lesson, let's follow Abraham's example and James' instructions by spending a little time praying for people around us and for our nation as a whole. If you are doing this study with a group, I encourage you to also spend time praying together. I have included a few passages that might assist you as you pray.

> Our prayers are just as powerful and effective as the prayers of Abraham.

<u>Pray for people you know are in need of healing or forgiveness</u>:

Psalm 103:1-5   Psalm 107:19-20   Isaiah 41:10

<u>Pray for your church and your church leaders</u>:

Ephesians 1:15-17   Colossians 1:9-12   Hebrews 12:1-3

<u>Pray for your nation and elected leaders</u>:

Psalm 33:12-22   2 Chronicles 7:14

Like Abraham, your faith has been credited to you as righteousness. Your prayers are powerful and effective.

WEEK FOUR | DAY FIVE

Personal Application

Application from Day One

In Day One, we reviewed the covenantal promise God made to Abraham and determined that, as believers in Jesus (Abraham's Seed), we are considered Abraham's spiritual descendants and heirs to the promise.

Look back at Genesis 15:6. What was attributed to Abraham as righteousness?

_____

According to Galatians 3:8, what did God announce in advance to Abraham?

_____

Interestingly, what did Jesus say about Abraham in John 8:56?

_____

As God helped Abraham understand the significance of His promise that "all nations would be blessed through [him]," the Patriarch recognized that God would save all nations through his Seed. That Seed was our Jesus. Abraham was saved by faith in Jesus.

> Abraham recognized that God would save all nations through his Seed. That Seed was our Jesus.

On the lines below, write Jesus' words as recorded in John 14:6:

_____

_____

Take a moment to praise our God for the consistency of His Word and to thank Him for the gift of His Son, Jesus, through whom the people of all nations can be saved.

Application from Day Two

Abraham was visited by three men. Look back at our Day Two lesson and note the likely identity of these mysterious visitors:

_____

Abraham was a gracious host to his heavenly visitors. I have to admit, hospitality is not one of my spiritual gifts. I am an introvert by nature. Entertaining is stressful for me because I am not very good at small talk and I feel a little over stimulated when there are a lot of conversations going on around me or music is playing while I am trying to talk. However, what do the following passages tell us about the importance of hospitality?

Romans 12:13 _____

Hebrews 13:2 _____

1 Peter 4:9 _____

It is possible 1 Peter 4:9 was written with people like me in mind, and I continue to push myself to be a better host. After all, when we are gracious and hospitable to strangers, we just might be hosting angels, as Abraham did.

Whether you thrive on entertaining at your home or struggle to think of something to say during a quiet dinner party, I encourage you to seek out opportunities to offer hospitality, not only to friends, but also to people you do not know very well. You will strengthen friendships, and, you never know, you just may show hospitality "to angels without knowing it."

> Seek out opportunities to offer hospitality, not only to friends, but also to people you do not know very well.

Application from Day Three

Abraham boldly persisted in prayer for the city his nephew called home. Although he was certainly passionate, he was not irreverent. God allowed Abraham to audaciously pray for the wicked city and there was no hint of irritation during the exchange.

Interestingly, there is another time when Scripture records someone's persistent prayer.

Read Luke 18:1-8.

According to verse 1, what was the reason Jesus told the disciples this parable?

_____

What do you learn about the importance of being diligent in prayer from the following passages?

Philippians 4:6 _____

Colossians 4:2 _____

When we come before our God with a burden on our hearts, as with Abraham, He is not irritated by our persistence in prayer. God made a point not to hide the impending destruction of Sodom and Gomorrah from Abraham (Genesis 18:17). He knew Abraham would make those bold requests on behalf of the cities. Our God also knows the concerns that weigh heavily upon your heart today, and I would be remiss if I did not give you an opportunity to talk to him about them. So, grab a fresh cup of coffee and get comfortable. Spend a few moments boldly petitioning our God. He delights in His relationship with you. Go ahead, be audacious. Be respectfully courageous. He might just bring about a merciful deliverance in your life.

> When we come before our God with a burden on our hearts, He is not irritated by our persistence in prayer.

Application from Day Four

As Lot and his family sprinted toward the town of Zoar, Mrs. Lot made the deadly mistake of turning a yearning eye back toward Sodom. As a result of her desire to preserve the past, she was turned into a pillar of salt that the historian Josephus recalls seeing thousands of years later during the first century A.D. As believers in Jesus, we have been delivered from our old lives and have become new creations.

According to Ephesians 4:22-24, what are we to put off and how are we made new?

_____

Now read Ephesians 4:25-32 and note some of the specifics we are to put off and put on in our new life as a believer in Christ?

Put Off: Put On:

_____   _____

_____   _____

_____   _____

_____   _____

_____   _____

_____   _____

If you are doing this study with a group, compare answers, which will vary, depending upon the versions of the Bible and interpretation of passages. As you peruse your lists, what is one negative attribute you have successfully put off?

_____

What Christ-like attributes have you successfully put on?

_____

As we close this week filled with destruction and consequences, celebrate your victories as a believer in Christ. Putting off that old self takes work. May Mrs. Lot's demise on her journey to a new life serve as a stark reminder to keep your eyes on Jesus and resist the temptation to look fondly back on any lifestyle or choice that is inconsistent with one who has been "created to be like God in true righteousness and holiness" (Ephesians 4:24).

Week 5

Opposing Offspring

WEEK FIVE | **DAY ONE**

Sordid Lineage

Let's get our father to drink wine and then sleep with him
and preserve our family line through our father.

GENESIS 19:32

As we begin another week as eyewitnesses to God's promises to Abraham, the cities of Sodom and Gomorrah are still smoldering. Mrs. Lot is preserved as a warning not to cherish a sinful lifestyle, and Abraham's nephew Lot and his daughters have fled to the neighboring town of Zoar. I would guess the now-widowed father was thankful his daughters escaped the catastrophe unharmed. However, even after the burning sulfur ceased, Lot still seemed to be grappling with some lingering fear.

According to Genesis 19:30, where did Lot and his daughters settle and what was the reason?

I find it interesting that Lot was originally too afraid to run to the mountains for shelter, as the angels suggested, but once he and his daughters were safely in Zoar, fear caused him to go to the extreme of making his dwelling in a mountain cave.

One of the Ferguson family's favorite vacation spots is in the Texas Hill Country, and we have often hiked in the area. Over the years, we walked inside a few caves and I cannot imagine the new Lot family home was anything but cold, dark, and somewhat depressing. Even if Lot's daughters covered the ground with handmade rugs and strategically placed pottery of various sizes and shapes around the gray stony walls, their home was still just a dark, damp cave. There were no windows through which to see the morning sunshine and no neighbors with which to converse. I would presume Lot's daughters were not happy cave-dwellers.

Please read Genesis 19:31-38.

According to verse 31, what circumstances motivated the older sister to come up with her sordid plan?

For women in that culture, the inability to bear children "was looked upon as a gnawing grief, and sometimes regarded as a sign of divine disfavor."[26] Childbearing was linked with a woman's value and it was her primary purpose in life. The only man around that cave was Lot. He had no other living children, and his girls apparently believed they were running out of time to begin their families and preserve their family line. Lot's daughters felt trapped in their circumstances, and it appears they not only lacked husbands, they also lacked boundaries.

> Lot's daughters felt trapped in their circumstances, and it appears they not only lacked husbands, they also lacked boundaries.

Look back at Genesis 19:6-8. What alternative had Lot offered all the men of Sodom when they demanded to have sex with the male visitors?

Lot's actions back in Sodom had not only communicated a lack of concern for his daughters' purity and wellbeing, he also conveyed an utter lack of respect for his daughters. Read the following passages and then write your thoughts about any correlation between the events at Lot's home in Sodom and the actions of his daughters in the cave:

Job 4:8   Proverbs 22:6   Galatians 6:7-8

_____

_____

_____

What did both verses 33 and 35 of Genesis 19 emphasize about Lot?

_____

Lot's daughters lacked respect for their father and did not seem to have any sense of healthy boundaries. From what you have learned about Sodom, how do you think the attitudes of the young women might have reflected the environment in which they were raised?

_____

_____

_____

WEEK FIVE

Please re-read Genesis 19:36-38. Other than references to Lot's descendants and the description of him as a righteous man in the book of 2 Peter, (mentioned in a previous lesson) this is the last information we have about Abraham's beloved nephew. We do not know how he responded when he discovered his daughters' scheme. Nothing is mentioned about his later years or his death. We can, however, get a little more information about the boys who were conceived on those consecutive nights in that cave.

What was the name of the son of the oldest daughter? _____

What was the name of the son of the younger daughter? _____

According to the footnote in my Bible, Moab sounds like the Hebrew for "from father" and Ben-Ammi means "son of my father's people."[27] As disturbing as the two young women's actions were there in the mountainous cave they called home, they did seem to be motivated by a desire to carry on their family line.

Moab's descendants settled at Ar, just east of the southern part of the Dead Sea,[28] and according to _The Moody Atlas of Bible Lands_,[29] the Ammonites settled in a small area northwest of that same sea. Years later, the Israelites (Abraham's descendants) passed through the region where the Moabites and Ammonites were living. According to Deuteronomy 2:9, 19, what did God tell the Israelites not to do, and what was the stated reason for those instructions?

_____

_____

God continued to be merciful to Lot (Genesis 19:16) as well as his descendants. Interestingly, look at the genealogy of Jesus, listed in Matthew chapter 1.

According to verse 5, who was the mother of Obed (and great-grandmother of King David)?

> God continued to be merciful to Lot as well as his descendants.

According to verse 7, which of Solomon's sons was an ancestor of Jesus?

_____

How is Ruth described in Ruth 1:4? _____

According to 1 King 14:21, who was the mother of Rehoboam and what was her heritage?

_____

Lot and his daughters were mercifully saved from the destruction of Sodom. Many generations later, God continued to be merciful toward Lot's descendants when He graciously chose to include each of the sons conceived by Lot and his misguided daughters in the lineage of the Savior of the world.

But God demonstrates his own love for us in this: While we were still sinners, Christ died for us. (Romans 5:8)

> God graciously chose to include each of the sons conceived by Lot and his misguided daughters in the lineage of the Savior of the world.

WEEK FIVE · DAY TWO

Mercy Triumphs

*. . . because judgment without mercy will be shown to anyone
who has not been merciful. Mercy triumphs over judgment.*

JAMES 2:13

After the destruction of Sodom, Gomorrah, and the other cities of the plain (Genesis 19:29), Abraham rose early in the morning, left his tent, and stood near the spot where he had last conversed with his Lord (Genesis 19:27). He thoughtfully looked down upon the smoldering remains of the city his nephew had called home. When Lot and his daughters went to live in the mountain cave, there is no indication in our Bibles that Abraham was contacted. It is possible the Lord reassured Abraham that Lot had been spared, and I presume the Patriarch heard about the demise of Lot's wife. After all, a woman preserved as a pillar of salt was not an everyday occurrence and certainly had to be a primary topic within in the community. Whether or not Abraham knew of Lot's escape, the fatherly uncle decided it was time to move on. His entourage packed up their tents and ventured into the region of the Negev.

To begin today's lesson, please read Genesis 20:1-2.

Gerar was located in the southwestern region of the Promised Land, near the coast of the Mediterranean Sea, in the land of the Philistines.[30] What familiar lie did Abraham perpetuate when he settled there?

_____

What once again happened to Sarah as a result of Abraham's deception?

_____

Please read Genesis 20:3-7. What do you learn about Sarah's participation in her husband's repetitive ruse (vs. 5)?

_____

I think it is interesting that Abimelek was not one of God's people, yet God clearly spoke to him in a dream. I also think the timing of this incident is noteworthy. When God destroyed the cities of the plain, which actually referred to five cities around Sodom (only Zoar was spared), we can safely assume the entire region heard about the catastrophic destruction. What question does King Abimelek ask God in his dream (vs. 4)?

_____

Abimelek appears to have had a healthy fear of God after recognizing his ability to rain down burning sulfur at will. The timing of Abimelek's intended courtship of Sarah was also significant for another reason. Look back at Genesis 18:14.

When did God say Sarah would have a son?

_____

If Abimelek had slept with Sarah even once during the time frame in which the Child of Promise was to be conceived, the legitimacy of Abraham's heir and the fulfillment of God's covenant promise would have been in question. Not to mention, if Sarah and Abraham were living apart, the pledged conception by Abraham and Sarah would not have been possible.

Now read Genesis 20:8-16.

According to verse 11, what assumption did Abraham make about Abimelek?

_____

Abimelek acted with a clear conscience, and God protected not only the king, but also Sarah, who had participated in the deception. Abraham knew the long-awaited child was to be born within the year. If I may be so bold, the timing of the future patriarch's deception gives the impression he was the one who held a somewhat lackadaisical attitude toward God and His promise. The Lord had been merciful toward Lot in Sodom, but He was also merciful toward Lot's uncle who had a propensity for deception.

> Abimelek acted with a clear conscience, and God protected not only the king, but also Sarah, who had participated in the deception.

How did God describe Abraham in verse 7?

_____

The Hebrew word used here is *nabi,* which means "spokesman" or "speaker."[31] It is comforting to know God works through imperfect people, but it can also be somewhat discouraging when we expect the Lord's servants to live up to the principles in God's Word. When they fail, as Abraham did, sometimes we are left feeling confused, betrayed, and deeply disappointed.

From Abimelek's words to Abraham, what evidence do you find that Abimelek was experiencing some of those same feelings?

_____

_____

WEEK FIVE

Have you ever noticed that those who are keenly aware of their own need for mercy are much more likely to extend it to others? God has shown me abundant mercy and yet, I have, at times, had difficulty extending mercy toward someone who I felt treated me unfairly or, even more so, someone who treated one of my family members unjustly.

Read the following verses and note what Jesus said about the importance of extending mercy.

Matthew 5:7 _____

Luke 6:36 _____

Romans 12:18 _____

Is there anyone to whom you need to extend mercy? If so, I encourage you to do so now. Make a phone call, walk over to your neighbor's home, or drive to a family member's house. Just as King Abimelek gave gifts to the one who had done things "that should never be done," do whatever you can to make things right and be at peace with anyone who has wronged you.

> Is there anyone to whom you need to extend mercy? If so, I encourage you to do so now.

Write your thoughts below:

_____

_____

What additional information does Genesis 20:13 provide about the consistency of Abraham and Sarah's deception?

We now know the topic of conversation as Abraham and Sarah left their hometown of Ur. This ruse was planned in advance, and the couple told this story everywhere they went. I am sure Sarah was hoping the incident with Abimelek would put an end to that risky lie. In an effort to make things right, the king not only offered slaves and livestock to Abraham, he offered to let the couple live in whatever land they wanted within his territory.

What was the reason Abimelek gave for paying Abraham a thousand shekels of silver (vs.16)?

To be vindicated means "to clear of accusation, censure, suspicion, etc."[32] What does the king's use of this word tell you about the way the people of Gerar and all of Abraham's household slaves probably viewed Sarah after she had once again been whisked off to become part of a foreign king's harem?

God had been merciful toward Abimelek, and the king had been merciful toward Abraham and Sarah. As we close our lesson, please read Genesis 20:17-18 and note what merciful act Abraham performed as God's prophet and spokesman.

> God had been merciful toward Abimelek, and the king had been merciful toward Abraham and Sarah.

Mercy triumphs over judgment. (James 2:13b)

WEEK FIVE **DAY THREE**

Complementary Laughter

*Now the Lord was gracious to Sarah as He had said,
and the Lord did for Sarah what He had promised.*

GENESIS 21:1

*I*have to admit, it has been a difficult month for the Fergusons. A close relative has been diagnosed with terminal cancer, and although we know God is sovereign and on His throne, our family is heartbroken. As if that were not enough for a family to endure, our young, vibrant daughter is dealing with some health issues of her own. To add to the chaos, her car was stolen two days ago while parked outside a friend's apartment. Can we just all agree that life is sometimes disappointing and stressful? What about you? What struggles have you endured lately that have caused you to feel disappointed, created stress, or possibly even made you wonder about the faithfulness of God?

> Can we just all agree that life is sometimes disappointing and stressful?

The first passages of Scripture we will read today are a reminder that God is indeed faithful. He operates on a timetable that does not always feel timely, and from our limited perspective, the struggles of this life sometimes feel purposeless. However, the Lord's ways are not our ways (Isaiah 55:8), and even when life is full of disappointments and stress, we can rest in the assurance that He "works out everything in conformity with the purpose of His will" (Ephesians 1:11) in due time.

As we begin our lesson today, due time had arrived for Abraham and Sarah. Their long season of disappointment had finally come to an end. The morning sunrise ushered in the arrival of the long-awaited Child of the Promise.

Please read Genesis 21:1-7.

Sometimes laughter is sweetest after a long season of sorrow. God brought Sarah laughter both through the name of her long-awaited son and by her awareness of His faithfulness to keep His Word.

> Sometimes laughter is sweetest after a long season of sorrow.

Do you sometimes wonder if God really will keep His Word? Let's look at a couple of scriptures we can hold onto during our seasons of disappointment or waiting. I could use the reminder today, and I trust you will find these passages encouraging, as well. Note the truths you can hold onto in each of these passages:

Deuteronomy 7:9 _____

Deuteronomy 31:6 _____

Psalm 89:8 _____

Isaiah 54:10 _____

Our Lord is a faithful God and even when the mountains seem to shake under the weight of life's disappointments, God's unfailing love for us will not be shaken loose. We are loved and our God keeps His Word, even when keeping His promise requires an old, barren woman to bear a child.

> God's unfailing love for us will not be shaken loose.

Look back at the struggles you noted at the beginning of today's lesson. Although you do not know the specifics of how God will bring you through these challenges, you can trust that He will indeed work out "everything in conformity with the purpose of His will" (Ephesians 1:11) in due time. So imagine with me for a moment that the struggle is behind you, and you have seen God's faithfulness through your trial. Let's thank God in advance of the resolution by turning Genesis 21:1 into a personal profession of thanks. Fill in the blanks below with your name and speak this personalized verse out loud to God as a prayer of praise.

> Let's thank God in advance by turning Genesis 21:1 into a personal profession of thanks.

Now the Lord was gracious to _____ *as He had said, and the Lord did for* _____ *what He had promised.*

God will keep His promises. You can count on that. According to Genesis 21:6, what did Sarah say people would do when they heard about Isaac's birth?

> God will keep His promises. You can count on that.

I would guess that everyone who knew Abraham and Sarah was aware of their lifelong desire to have a child together. The circumstances surrounding the birth of Isaac ("He Laughs") were such that everyone who heard about him would join Sarah in laughing with delight. If you feel comfortable and are doing this study with a group, share the struggles you wrote in today's lesson with them. Pray together, and when God somehow works in your circumstances, laugh with delight together as you celebrate His faithfulness. The moments when we see God's undeniable activity in our lives should be cherished and celebrated, because when the normal routines, challenges, and demands of life inevitably return, memories of God's faithfulness increase our faith that He will be faithful in the future.

> The moments when we see God's undeniable activity in our lives should be cherished and celebrated.

Re-read Genesis 17:11-13. What were God's instructions regarding males born in Abraham's household?

Abraham and Sarah had their promised son, and Isaac was circumcised on the eighth day, just as God commanded. However, once the celebrations and ceremonies were over, the couple had to return to everyday life. Hagar and Ishmael were still around, and the arrival of the long-awaited child of the promise only complicated the dynamics of the blended families living within the tents of Abraham's household.

Please read Genesis 21:8-10.

According to verse 9, what was Ishmael doing at Isaac's weaning celebration?

One of the definitions of the word "mock" is "to ridicule by imitation; mimic derisively." I am guessing that any of you with an older brother or those who have raised a few sons can picture this scene in vivid detail. Isaac was the center of attention at this feast. I would guess there was talk about God's "everlasting covenant with [Isaac's] descendants" (Genesis 17:19). Everyone was celebrating the birth of Abraham's long-awaited child of the promise, and Ishmael was the one who was now laughing—not with delight at the mercy of God, as his father had—but with strong feelings of contempt for the son who would be the heir to all of God's covenant promises. Ishmael was envious, and Sarah was furious.

What did Sarah ask Abraham to do (vs. 10)? _____

Hagar's son had been Sarah's idea (Genesis 16:2). The fact is, when we take matters into our own hands and attempt to make God's plans come to pass our way, we can expect to endure consequences. Now that God's long-awaited promise had been fulfilled, Sarah wanted to eliminate those consequences from her life.

> When we take matters into our own hands and attempt to make God's plans come to pass our way, we can expect to endure consequences.

Read Genesis 21:11-13.

How did Sarah's request impact Abraham?

_____

What did God tell Abraham to do and what assurances did He once again make about Ishmael?

_____

Isaac was the child through whom the Seed, which is ultimately Jesus Christ, would come. Ishmael was loved by God and loved by Abraham, but it was time for the two boys to live apart. Sarah may have been eliminating the sibling rivalry within her tents, but her rogue plan to start a family through Hagar resulted in the heartrending loss of a beloved son for her husband.

> Isaac was the child through whom the Seed, which is ultimately Jesus Christ, would come.

Isaac was appropriately named "He Laughs," for laughter surrounded him both before his birth and in his early years of life. Abraham had laughed with delight, as did everyone who heard of the circumstances of his birth. His mother had laughed in disbelief at the promise of a child in her old age. The son who knew the family inheritance would be passed to his younger half-brother laughed with contempt as Isaac took his God-ordained place in the family as the firstborn child of Abraham and Sarah and heir to the covenant promises of a faithful God. The birth of the one so appropriately named "He Laughs" was indeed the impetus for much laughter.

WEEK FIVE | DAY FOUR

Emotional Acts of Faith

*Early the next morning Abraham took some food and a skin of water
and gave them to Hagar. He set them on her shoulders
and then sent her off with the boy.*

GENESIS 21:14A

*I*n yesterday's lesson, Sarah insisted Abraham "get rid of" Hagar and Ishmael, and God confirmed that the mother and son should indeed be sent to live elsewhere. I doubt Abraham got much sleep that night, and I imagine his heart was heavy as he got out of bed early the next morning.

Begin today by re-reading Genesis 21:8-13.

According to verse 11, how did Abraham feel about Sarah's insistence that Hagar and Ishmael be sent away?

Read Genesis 21:14 and imagine you are watching this intense, agonizing moment in the life of our big-hearted protagonist.

What did Abraham send along with Hagar and Ishmael?

Abraham lovingly prepared provisions for Hagar and Ishmael. Although he knew the mother and son had to leave, he must have been overcome with emotion. In fact, according to *The New American Commentary,* in the original language of the text, the anguish of that moment is captured by the awkwardness of the Hebrew in verse 14. "Mention of 'the boy' is delayed in the sentence so as to suggest that the transference of the boy from Abraham's hand to [Hagar's] is undertaken at the last possible moment."[33]

When our youngest child and only daughter, Brianna, first attended Montessori pre-school, this momma's heart was aching before we ever arrived at the property. My girl's graduation to this new phase of life meant the end of a parenting season. To add to the depth of my emotions, on the way into the classroom, Brianna locked her arms around the back of my neck, wrapped her pudgy little legs tightly around my waist, and determined that she was not going to be left in that school building. As the teacher smiled sweetly and tried to pry her limbs loose and take her into the classroom, Bri wailed and sobbed and clung to me even more tightly. By that time, I had tears streaming down my own face and wanted to return to my car and take my baby girl right back home, never to return. However, I knew attending pre-school was best for Brianna. So, I kissed her cheek, hugged her tightly, affirmed my love for her, and then smiled reassuringly as the teacher whisked her off (still screaming) into the classroom. I looked down at the floor as I quickly made my way down the school hallway, out the door, and back into my car, where I immediately burst into tears.

I am sure Abraham was much more dignified than this emotional mother was on my youngest child's first morning of pre-school, but I would guess his emotions were probably similarly raw as he packed the food and skin of water on Hagar's shoulders and then hugged his son one last time. A season in Abraham's life was passing as he sent his son off—not for a few hours—but for the rest of his life. Perhaps, as the Hebrew suggests, Abraham was the one who clung tightly to his son, released his grip at the last possible moment, and turned away quickly in an effort to control his emotions. It could not have been easy, but Abraham obeyed God's instructions and trusted Him to care for Ishmael and make him into a great nation, just as He promised (Genesis 17:20).

> A season in Abraham's life was passing as he sent his son off—not for a few hours—but for the rest of his life.

Have you ever had to say an emotional goodbye to a close friend or family member? Whether the separation was to be short or lengthy, what insight does your experience provide as you consider the emotions Abraham, Hagar, and Ishmael might have been feeling as they said their goodbyes?

> Have you ever had to say an emotional goodbye to a close friend or family member?

Let's see what happened as Hagar and Ishmael ventured into the desert. Please read Genesis 21:15-21. Look closely at verses 16-17. Who was crying?

_____ and _____

The water was gone, mother and son were wandering in the desert, and at some point Ishmael began to cry, probably overcome with grief at the loss of his father and from the effects of dehydration in the dry desert of Beersheba. Hagar, unable to bear the thought of watching her son die of thirst, lovingly tucked him under the shelter of a desert shrub and distanced herself from her son enough to allow her own emotions to erupt to the surface.

According to verse 17, the angel acknowledged Hagar's tears as he assured her that God heard her son crying as well. God hears—Ishmael. Look back at God's words to Hagar in Genesis 16:11. What was the reason God gave her son the name Ishmael?

_____

As the mother and son wandered in the desert, feeling desperate and assuming all hope of survival was lost, God reassured Hagar by reminding her that He not only heard of her misery, as He had the last time she was alone in the desert, but He heard her son crying as he lay there, feeling abandoned, seemingly dying from thirst. Our God hears. When our circumstances seem hopeless and we feel utterly alone and forgotten, we can rest assured our God is aware of the misery we experience in this life, and He is somehow at work in our circumstances.

> We can rest assured our God is aware of the misery we experience in this life, and He is somehow at work in our circumstances.

What did Jesus say about God in John 5:17? _____

How does the awareness that God is always at work encourage you personally at this time?

_____

_____

God will never leave us or forsake us (Hebrews 13:5). He is a God who hears of our misery, and He is always at His work (John 5:17). As Hagar sobbed in the desert because of her son's suffering, she was completely unaware of a well

> God will never leave us or forsake us (Hebrews 13:5).

full of water—God's answer to her prayers and the life-sustaining provision she and Ishmael so desperately needed—located right there in her vicinity that day in the desert.

What instructions did the angel give Hagar in Genesis 21:18?

_____

According to verse 19, when did God make Hagar aware of the well that had been right there the entire time?

_____

Sometimes when we are most discouraged, we have difficulty recognizing God's answers to our prayers. Hagar was in a state of utter despair. She was so focused on the lack of water in her goat-skin canteen that she was completely unaware of the well right there in plain view. As soon as she took her eyes off what she lacked and trusted God enough to lift her son up and take him by the hand in order to continue their journey by faith, she was able to see God's provision that had been there the entire time.

> Sometimes when we are most discouraged, we have difficulty recognizing God's answers to our prayers.

What is your empty goat-skinned canteen right now? Take a moment to pray and ask God if there is some act of faith you need to take in order to force your focus off of that which you lack, and take the next step in your journey by faith, so you are able to see His provision for you more clearly?

_____

God is faithful and He is worthy of your trust. Even if you feel abandoned or are experiencing a heartrending loss, if you will take your eyes off what you lack, do your best to put one foot in front of the other, and continue your journey, trusting God for your every need, you will somehow see His provision and you just might discover, as Hagar did, the answer to your prayers has been in plain view all along.

> God is faithful and He is worthy of your trust.

WEEK FIVE | **DAY FIVE**

Personal Application

Application from Day One

What a week! In Day One's lesson, Lot's daughters carried out a despicable plot of deception and manipulation as they got their father drunk and took advantage of his incapacitated state in order to carry on their dysfunctional family line. I must say, as awful as the girls' behavior was, it occurs to me that their father probably had a drinking problem. It never seemed to enter the girls' minds that their father would not overindulge. Lot's weakness became a part of his family legacy as the story of his grandsons' manipulative conceptions were passed from generation to generation and made their way to the pages of Scripture.

Rest assured, if you have children, they are aware of your weaknesses and those weaknesses will become a part of your legacy if left unchecked. As your children grow up in your home and interact with you on a daily basis, they instinctively learn how to exploit your weaknesses. Think back to your own upbringing. Did you or your siblings ever take advantage of your parents' weaknesses? If so, give an example:

> Rest assured, if you have children, they are aware of your weaknesses and those weaknesses will become a part of your legacy if left unchecked.

_____

_____

_____

Now take a moment to examine your current relationship with your parents and/or your children. What is one change you can make today that would enable your family interactions to be healthier and prevent any weaknesses or manipulative tendencies from becoming a part of your family heritage?

_____

Take a moment to ask God to help you make that change, and then start working on it today. Your legacy is at stake.

Application from Day Two

Speaking of weaknesses, look back at our Day Two lesson this week. With what weakness did Abraham apparently struggle? (Read Genesis 20, if you need to refresh your memory.)

Abraham's deceptive tendencies remind us that God uses flawed people. Our Lord is merciful toward us. He created us and He knows how we are formed; He remembers that we are dust (Psalm 103:14). God's mercy is evident whenever He chooses to bless us or use us, despite our weaknesses. As with Abraham, understanding the depth of God's mercy inspires us be merciful toward others. Abimelek was merciful toward Abraham, and Abraham, in turn, was merciful to Abimelek, praying for the king's household so God would heal and restore their fruitfulness.

> Abraham's deceptive tendencies remind us that God uses flawed people.

Is there someone you need to pray for today? Are you harboring unforgiveness toward someone who has deceived you or embarrassed you, or wounded your heart? Follow Abimelek and Abraham's example. Choose to forgive and do what you can to make things right. Take a few minutes right now to sincerely pray for a specific need that person's household might have at this time. If there is sickness, pray for healing; if there is bitterness, pray for peace; if there is a damaged reputation, pray for restoration. Be specific and pray God will be generous to this person. After all, as a believer in Christ, God has shown you tremendous mercy. Regardless what sins or offenses you have committed, Christ died for you (Romans 5:8).

> Is there someone you need to pray for today?

For whom are you praying (It is alright to write in code!): _____

What is one specific need for which you are praying? _____

Application from Days Three and Four

As I consider how we might personally apply the passages we read about Isaac and Ishmael this week, I think it might be more important to discuss how we should *not* apply these passages.

There are some verses in Scripture that are descriptive. They describe events that took place so we can better understand the flow of a story and gain understanding of the context. Other passages are prescriptive, and although they addressed a situation at a certain time in biblical history, they serve as examples for us to follow and contain principles that can also be applied to our lives today.

Re-read Genesis 21:8-14 and summarize what happened in your own words:

_____

_____

These passages about Abraham, Hagar, and Ishmael are descriptive, not prescriptive. God is not prescribing separation or divorce in order to stop children in blended families from arguing, and these passages do not give fathers permission to abandon their children.

To gain a better understanding of God's prescription for a godly father, let's take a few minutes to see what instruction fathers can find from other passages in our Bibles.

What does Ephesians 6:4 indicate fathers should do for their children?

_____

Look up 1 Timothy 5:8 and note what this passage says about those who do not provide for the members of their household, which would certainly include children.

_____

> These passages about Abraham, Hagar, and Ishmael are descriptive, not prescriptive.

> God's plan is for fathers and mothers to raise their children, teach them His ways, and provide for their needs as they grow and develop and mature.

God's plan is for fathers and mothers to raise their children, teach them His ways, and provide for their needs as they grow and develop and mature. The circumstances surrounding the births of Ishmael and Isaac were unique, and God's plan was specific.

Most of us know children who have either been abandoned by their fathers or whose fathers have failed to adequately provide for them physically, emotionally, or perhaps both. To end our week's lessons, please take a few moments to pray for those children. But as a means of application, I also want to encourage you to do something tangible for the needs of a child without an actively engaged father in his or her life. It has been my experience that if you ask a mother, who is doing her best to raise a child by herself, if there is some need her son(s) or daughter(s) have that is not being met, after she stops crying, she will be able to give you some ideas.

Do not feel obligated to try to meet these needs by yourself. If you are doing this study with a group, pool resources, share ideas, and consider working together to meet a need. If you are not studying with a group, make your church aware of the need or pool resources with a friend.

Just as was the case with Hagar, a single mom cannot bear to see her children do without. I am praying right now that your actions will show that single mom and her child(ren) that *God hears* them and is aware of their misery and their struggles. May that family take their eyes off of their empty goat-skinned canteens and see your kindness as God's faithful provision.

Write a brief summary of your experience:

_____

_____

_____

_____

Week 6

Refining Revelations

Well of the Oath

So that place was called Beersheba [Well of the Oath],
because the two men swore an oath there.

GENESIS 21:31

As we open our Bibles together this week, Ishmael is now married and he and his Egyptian wife are living in the Desert of Paran with his mother (Genesis 21:21). The promised child, Isaac, is now the only remaining son in Abraham and Sarah's tent. The Patriarch and his now-smaller family are still living in King Abimelek's territory in Philistine, and the king, accompanied by his military commander, makes an understandable request of Abraham.

Please read Genesis 21:22-23.

According to verse 22, what had Abimelek concluded about Abraham?

What did Abimelek ask Abraham to swear before God?

From what we have studied about Abraham, what do you think prompted Abimelek to make this request? (If you need to refresh your memory, re-read Genesis 20)

The old saying, "Fool me once, shame on you; fool me twice, shame on me" comes to mind. Abimelek recognized that God was with Abraham. He did not doubt that. But he also knew from experience that Abraham had a tendency to be deceptive. Abimelek wanted assurances from Abraham that he would be honest in all of their future dealings. The king wanted to make sure his household would never again become subject to God's wrath simply because he had been duped. Abimelek also knew he and his family would continue to interact with his formerly disingenuous neighbor, and he wanted Abraham to take an oath, swearing before God that he would never again deal falsely with the king or any of his descendants.

Being deceived or betrayed is an experience you do not easily forget. When our family decided to add a Yorkshire terrier to our household, we wanted to get our new furry family member from a private breeder rather than a pet store. Being inexperienced at purchasing a pet, we found a precious little puppy on a local breeder's website and were thrilled to read that her mother weighed less than five pounds and her father weighed in at seven pounds. The black and brown cutie was being offered for $450.00, which seemed appropriate for what is often referred to as a "Tea Cup Yorkie." I should have been concerned when the breeder offered to meet us somewhere instead of having us come to her home. When we met at a gas station parking lot, I had additional warning signs that all was not well when her husband kept rushing her to leave. But we had driven for over an hour, and the little puppy immediately began cuddling my daughter's neck. Feeling less than assured, we drove home with the darling new member of our family, Mollie. The next day, however, Mollie had a seizure while she was cuddling with my daughter. We rushed our new pet to the vet and had to immediately put her on medication. The vet also broke the news that she appeared to have allergies, and based on her age and size, our Yorkie would probably grow to about 14 pounds, not the 5-7 advertised on the breeder's website. Upon arriving back home, I immediately tried to get in touch with the women who met us at the gas station. Her website was no longer active and she did not return my calls. We never did receive those American Kennel

Club papers we were promised. Mollie is now eight years old and weighs a whopping 17 pounds. Thankfully, she has outgrown her seizure disorder, but she is allergic to grass and wheat and gets sick if she eats anything other than her special order, very expensive dog food. However, Mollie is a treasured member of the Ferguson family, and while she is definitely not a "Tea Cup Yorkie," my husband, Mark, affectionately calls her our "17-Pound, Bucket Yorkie." Needless to say, our entire family is much more cautious with our online purchases, and I would personally recommend you carefully check out a breeder before buying a pet.

Have you ever been deceived? If so, what lessons did you learn from the experience?

_____

_____

_____

Abimelek learned Abraham's God is powerful and made the wise decision to rely upon God to keep Abraham honest. According to Genesis 21:24, how did Abraham respond to Abimelek's request to make an oath that he would not deal falsely with Abimelek in the future?

> Abimelek learned Abraham's God is powerful and made the wise decision to rely upon God to keep Abraham honest.

Interestingly, after taking this oath, there is no record in Scripture of Abraham ever being deceptive again. It appears Abraham not only fulfilled his vow to deal honestly with Abimelek and his descendants, but, perhaps, while taking that oath, he was convicted to deal honestly with everyone else, as well.

Please read Genesis 21:25-30.

What was Abraham complaining about in verse 25?

_____

According to verse 27, what did the two men do after Abraham gave Abimelek the sheep and cattle?

_____

The Hebrew word translated as "treaty" in this verse is *Byrith*. It conveys the idea of cutting. *Strong's Concordance* defines it as "a compact (. . . made by passing between pieces of flesh); —confederacy, covenant, league."

As you read that definition, did you recall the covenant God "cut" with Abraham (Genesis 15)? Abimelek asked the Patriarch to make a vow to God that he would never again deal deceptively with him, but Abraham had a vow he wanted Abimelek to make as well. Abraham had dug a well in Abimelek's country where water was scarce. He wanted the rights to that well. We do not know the specific terms of the treaty, or covenant, these two men made, but as the Patriarch cut those sheep and cattle in two, I have to believe he reflected upon that one-sided covenant God made with him, guaranteeing that the land and the promised child would one day be his. God had been faithful to keep His Word. As Abraham and Abimelek walked through the pieces of the slain animals and agreed to a peaceful, honest relationship in which Abraham would live in Gerar and maintain the rights to the well his servants dug there, Abraham secured his first piece of the Promised Land. Abraham had been blessed with Isaac, and now, he also had the rights to a well. By means of their treaty, Abraham was being a blessing (Genesis 12:2) as he promised to treat Abimelek with kindness.

Once again, the word translated as "kindness" in verse 23 is the Hebrew word *hesed*. Abraham was beginning to fulfill his calling to be a blessing as he promised—made a covenant, guaranteeing it—to show God's goodness and kindness to Abimelek. He promised to treat the king with the same kindness with which God treats His covenant people.

> Abraham was beginning to fulfill his calling to be a blessing.

Read Genesis 21:31-33.

Why was that place at the well named Beersheba (vs. 31), and what did Abraham plant there?

By what name did Abraham call God in verse 33?

A Tamarisk tree is an evergreen tree.[34] Abraham considered this treaty, allowing him to live in Canaan and own that well, to be evidence of God's everlasting covenant promises being fulfilled.

As a way of closing our lesson today, re-read Genesis 17:7-19, and, if you are comfortable writing in your Bible, underline every occurrence of the word "everlasting."

I will establish my covenant as an everlasting covenant between me and you and your descendants after you for the generations to come, to be your God and the God of your descendants after you. (Genesis 17:7)

WEEK SIX DAY TWO

A Revelatory Test

Abraham reasoned that God could even raise the dead,
and so in a manner of speaking he did receive Isaac back from death.

HEBREWS 11:19

braham lived in Beersheba, in the land of the Philistines, for a long time (Genesis 21:34). We do not know the number of years, and we are not given any other details about the daily lives of our protagonist and his less-than-youthful wife, Sarah. We do not know much about the early years of Isaac's life. All we know is Abraham and Sarah stayed in the land of the Philistines with their son of promise, living by the well of the oath, both of which served as witnesses that Abraham's Eternal God is faithful.

Begin today by reading Genesis 22:1-2.

What did God instruct Abraham to do?

_____

Where was the sacrifice to take place?

_____

This had to be a shock to Abraham. Isaac was the only son Abraham had left. He was Abraham's evidence of God's faithfulness. He was the son through whom God promised to make Abraham's descendants as numerous as the stars in the sky (Genesis 15:5). God had promised to also establish His covenant with Isaac as an everlasting covenant for his descendants after him (Genesis 17:19). How could this be?

> Isaac was Abraham's evidence of God's faithfulness.

If you were in Abraham's position, with what thoughts do you think you would have been wrestling as you heard God's instructions?

_____

_____

_____

Abraham is considered the father of the Hebrew nation. He is the Patriarch of the Jewish faith. He is listed among the heroes of faith in Hebrews, chapter 11. But Abraham was human, just like you and me. We have seen in the past that he was an emotional man who questioned God and grieved over his childless state. He even lied when he thought his life might be in danger. I am going to guess Abraham did not sleep well that night. Perhaps he tossed and turned and cried out to God in an attempt to reconcile the request with all of God's previous promises. We do not know the process, but by early the next morning, this legendary man of faith exited his tent with an unwavering resolve to trust his God.

> Abraham was human, just like you and me.

Read Genesis 22:3 slowly and try to picture this scene as it unfolds through this verse of Scripture. What task did Abraham perform after he loaded his donkey, and who was with him?

_____

Abraham had gathered provisions to say goodbye to a son before. This time, while he loaded the donkey with enough food and water for their three-day journey, I imagine his heart was heavy and his words were few. Each blow of the ax, each piece of wood that he cut, must have solidified the reality of God's unfathomable request. I doubt Abraham was much of a conversationalist as the foursome made their way to Mount Moriah.

Please read Genesis 22:4-5. What insight into Abraham's state of mind do you gain from his use of the plural pronoun "we" when he spoke to his servants?

_____

Let's see what happened as Abraham and Isaac went up onto Mount Moriah. Please read Genesis 22:6-10.

What did Isaac notice as he and his father made their way up onto the mountain?

_____

Imagine that ominous background music I mentioned earlier in the study, once again playing in the background. Isaac had no idea he was the lamb for that burnt offering. What was Abraham's response (vs. 8)?

_____

Please read Hebrews 11:17-19 and summarize Abraham's thoughts as he laid Isaac—his beloved son of promise—on top of that wood and reached resolutely for the knife.

_____

_____

That is faith. Write the definition of faith as recorded in Hebrews 11:1:

_____

_____

Abraham had confidence that God would somehow bring Isaac back from the dead and even though he had no idea why God would make such a request, by faith, he felt completely assured that his son, through whom all of God's promises would be fulfilled, would somehow be returned to him. That confident assurance enabled him to obey God's unexplainable request. Faith is evident by one's actions.

> Abraham had confidence that God would somehow bring Isaac back from the dead

Read James 2:21-23 and then describe how Abraham's actions on that mountain in Moriah revealed his faith:

_____

_____

Although this was the greatest test of Abraham's faith, we have watched as his faith has grown and developed throughout his journey with God. Read each of the following passages from Hebrews 11, and note the actions he took that revealed his faith:

Hebrews 11:8: _____

Hebrews 11:9: _____

Hebrews 11:17-18: _____

Abraham's faith and his actions were working together all along his journey. As James said, "faith by itself, if it is not accompanied by action, is dead" (James 2:17). Abraham was tested, and if we were grading him, he would have received an A+.

Please read Genesis 22:9-12.

As I read God's words to Abraham, I thought of the tests the Emergency Broadcast System occasionally performs through our television networks. The loud, extended beep sound is followed by the words "This is a test. This is only a test." Thankfully, this was indeed only a test. God never intended for Abraham to actually sacrifice his son.

> Although this was the greatest test of Abraham's faith, we have watched as his faith has grown and developed throughout his journey with God.

Abraham's faith and devotion to God had been revealed through his willingness to offer his treasured son of promise as a sacrifice to God. The Lord had given Abraham the gift of a son, and now it was clear Abraham was more devoted to the Giver than to the gift.

Is there any gift you treasure or hold so tightly that you are unwilling to release it to the Gift-Giver? If so, what fear is undermining your faith?

_____

_____

We will finish the story of Abraham's test on the mountain in Moriah in Day Three's lesson. Between now and then, ask God to reveal anything you are clinging to more tightly than our Lord. Is there anything you are withholding from Him? What might be revealed by a test of your faith?

WEEK SIX — DAY THREE

The Lord Will Provide

So Abraham called that place The Lord Will Provide.
And to this day it is said, "On the mountain of the Lord it will be provided."

GENESIS 22:14

At the end of our last lesson, we left Abraham standing over his son Isaac with knife drawn, as the angel of the Lord stopped him from plunging it into his boy at the last possible second. To refresh your memory, re-read Genesis 22:9-12 and note what was revealed about Abraham during his test (vs.12):

_____

_____

It is difficult to imagine the relief Abraham must have felt when the angel stopped him from sacrificing his son. And Isaac? He had not been privy to his father's previous conversation with the Lord. He thought he was just going off to sacrifice a lamb as they had obviously done before. He must have been utterly confused and shocked when his father instead bound him and lay him upon that altar, then grabbed the knife with the intent to make *him* the sacrifice.

> It is difficult to imagine the relief Abraham must have felt when the angel stopped him from sacrificing his son.

111

Now read Genesis 22:13-19.

God indeed provided "the lamb for the burnt offering" (Genesis 22:8), just as Abraham said He would, and, in essence, Abraham received Isaac back from the dead (Hebrews 11:19), just as the faith-filled patriarch reasoned would happen on that mountain. Through his many experiences along his journey with God, our protagonist had grown to the point where he so feared and trusted God that he was even willing to sacrifice his beloved son of promise, if that is what the Lord asked of him.

Whether your relationship with God is new or you, like Abraham, have followed Him for years and persevered through many challenging events in your life, how have your experiences strengthened your faith in our Lord?

> How have your experiences strengthened your faith in our Lord?

_____

_____

_____

Abraham had grown into a man of unwavering faith. He did not just believe God would fulfill His promises, Abraham *knew* God would fulfill His promises. Look at Genesis 22:17-18, and finish writing out each of the promises God once again confirmed He would be faithful to fulfill.

1). I will surely _____

2). I will make your descendants _____

_____

3). Your descendants will take possession of _____

4). Through your offspring (Seed) all nations _____

Abraham witnessed the flaming torch and smoking fire-pot (representing God's presence) pass through the slain animal pieces, guaranteeing His promises would come true. It was a one-sided covenant, and Abraham did not have to wonder whether his descendants (as numerous as the stars in the sky) would one day possess the land of Canaan or whether all nations would be blessed through

> God took opportunity to once again confirm His promises to Abraham.

his obedience to God. Yes, knowing we human beings are prone to second guess, God took this opportunity to once again confirm His promises to Abraham. See, as Abraham stood over Isaac with that knife, his willingness to sacrifice his beloved son foreshadowed God's willingness to sacrifice His beloved Son, Jesus.

In fact, look again at Galatians 3:8 and note what God shared with Abraham:

We do not know for sure when God explained the full magnitude of the gospel to Abraham, but the moment God provided that ram in the thicket to be sacrificed as an atonement for sin rather than Isaac would have been an ideal time.

To atone means "to cover over, atone, propitiate, pacify. Most uses of the word . . . involve the theological meaning of 'covering over,' often with the blood of a sacrifice in order to atone for some sin."[35]

What does Hebrews 10:3-4 tell you about the atoning power of the animal sacrifices, such as Abraham was offering, or which were later prescribed in God's law?

Hold your place in Hebrews, chapter 10. We are coming right back, but first, turn back to Genesis 22:2 and note the location of the mountain where Abraham was willing to offer his son as a sacrifice:

According to 2 Chronicles 3:1, where was Mount Moriah located?

Abraham stood with knife drawn over his beloved son, Isaac, in the region of Moriah, which was somewhere near Jerusalem. Thousands of years later, God's gospel—His plan of salvation—came to fruition as Jesus, God's beloved Son, was also offered up near Jerusalem (John 19:20) as the atoning sacrifice for all nations on earth.

Now turn back to Hebrews 10 and read verses 5-10. How did Jesus respond to God when it was time for Him to come to earth as our atoning sacrifice (vs. 9)?

WEEK SIX

Look back at Genesis 22:11. How did Abraham respond when the angel called his name?

_____

"Here I am." That is the way a person of unwavering faith responds to the call of our God. He is a promise keeper. He is worthy of our trust. He provided a ram in the thicket to save Isaac. He provided our Jesus to permanently and fully atone for our every sin. As Abraham's descendants through faith in Abraham's Seed—Jesus Christ (Galatians 3:16)—we, along with people of every tribe and language and people and nation (Revelation 5:9) are blessed to experience God's kindness and goodness as He saved us with the atoning blood of Jesus when He was crucified on a mountain near Jerusalem. Indeed, "on the mountain of the Lord it [was] provided" (Genesis 22:14).

> "Here I am." That is the way a person of unwavering faith responds to the call of our God.

WEEK SIX | DAY FOUR

The Divine Orchestrator

*We are confident that God is able to orchestrate everything
to create something good and beautiful when we love Him
and accept His invitation to live according to His plan.*

ROMANS 8:28 (VOICE)

In Day Three's lesson, we see Abraham had been willing to sacrifice his son—the one through whom God had promised to fulfill His covenant. Abraham's willingness to offer up Isaac was a foreshadowing of God's willingness to sacrifice His Son, Jesus, to atone for the sins of all the world for all time. God is always at work (John 5:17), and His plan to save the world through His Son was the main focus of everything He chose to have recorded in Scripture. In fact, Jesus' crucifixion was not only illustrated through Abraham's willingness to sacrifice Isaac on Mount Moriah, it was portrayed over and over again through the animal sacrifices that God would later require as part of His law governing Abraham's descendants.

Look again at 2 Chronicles 3:1. What significant structure was later built on Mount Moriah?

_____

Abraham stood on a mountain which was in the same general location in Jerusalem where the regular temple sacrifices would later take place. Read Leviticus 9:7 and note the purpose for the sin offerings and burnt offerings that were performed there:

_____

The sacrifices prescribed by the law only covered sin. The sacrifices had to be offered regularly, year after year. "Day after day every priest [stood] and perform[ed] his religious duties; again and again he [offered] the same sacrifices, which [could] never take away sins" (Hebrews 10:11).

Now read Hebrews 10:1-4. According to verse 3, of what were the temple sacrifices an annual reminder?

> Abraham stood on a mountain which was in the same general location in Jerusalem where the regular temple sacrifices would later take place.

WEEK SIX

_____

What further insight into the purpose of the law (and the sacrifices) do you gain from Romans 3:19-20?

_____

_____

God's law, which he gave the people through the prophet, Moses, outlined God's expectations for His people, and although Genesis is considered to be part of the law, or Pentateuch (the first five books of the Bible), the law was represented by the Ten Commandments and is outlined primarily in Exodus, Leviticus, Numbers, and Deuteronomy. The purpose of

God's law was to make His people aware of their sin—which is simply a term describing acts and behaviors that do not meet God's expectations.

Now read Romans 7:7 and summarize it in your own words below:

_____

_____

_____

> God is the Divine Orchestrator. He illustrated His plan to save the entire world through the atoning sacrifice of His Son, Jesus.

The law and temple sacrifices were established to make people aware of our need for a savior. God is the Divine Orchestrator. He "works out everything in conformity with the purpose of His will" (Ephesians 1:11) and illustrated His plan to save the entire world through the atoning sacrifice of His Son, Jesus, over and over again as the people sacrificed innocent animals in the temple. The blood of the innocent covered the sins of the guilty.

How is Jesus described in John 1:29? _____

The sins of the whole world were atoned for when Jesus, the "Seed" of Abraham and the true "Lamb of God," was sacrificed in the region of Moriah, near Jerusalem. And God announced the gospel to Abraham in advance when He said, "All nations will be blessed through you" (Galatians 3:8).

After Abraham sacrificed that ram that had been caught in the thicket, God reiterated to His patriarch that "all nations on earth would be blessed" because of his obedience. Abraham and Isaac then returned to the servants who were waiting on them at the base of the mountain, just as Abraham said they would, and they all returned to Beersheba, where we are told Abraham stayed (Genesis 22:19).

Interestingly, following the recording of that epic event in Moriah, God, through inspiration of His Holy Spirit during the writing of Genesis, saw fit to include information at the end of Genesis, chapter 22, which at first glance seems to include completely unrelated details about the sons of Abraham's brother, Nahor.

Please read Genesis 22:20-24.

Okay, maybe I could just use a little comic relief after the very serious material we have been studying the past couple of days, but I could not help but chuckle as I read the names of Nahor's first two sons. What were their names?

_____ and _____

Who names their sons Uz and Buz? Can you just imagine the ribbing two brothers with those names would receive in a modern-day school room? I looked up both names in my Strong's Concordance, wondering if, perhaps, there was some significance to those names. It does not appear there was any significance to the names; just a father and mother who must have thought those were good names for their first two sons. Maybe they just wanted to keep the names short and easy to remember. Speaking of short, let's get back to the relevance of this seemingly random information at the end of Genesis 22 so this lesson does not become unnecessarily long.

Review the chart below, created from information contained in Genesis 11:29 and 22:20-23. Read those passages and write in the name of Bethuel's daughter below.

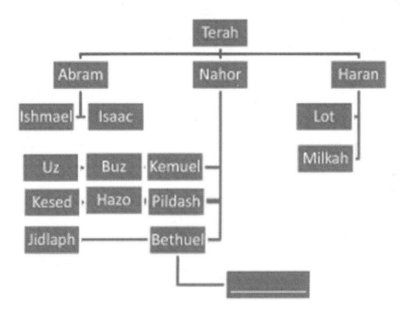

Now skip ahead for a moment. We will discover in Week Seven that Abraham sent his servant back to Mesopotamia to get a wife for Isaac (Genesis 24). According to Genesis 24:24, who was this young woman?

Now read Genesis 24:50-51. What did Laban (Rebekah's brother) and Bethuel say when Abraham's servant asked permission to take Rebekah back to become Isaac's wife?

God is the divine orchestrator. While Abraham's obedience to God was setting into motion God's plan of salvation through Abraham's Seed, God was also at work back in Mesopotamia, preparing a young woman to become Isaac's bride. Rebecca would give birth to the next generation of this promised lineage. Our God is always working (John 5:17), and He was orchestrating something "good and beautiful" as Abraham chose to "love Him and accept His invitation to live according to His plan" (Romans 8:28 VOICE).

WEEK SIX   DAY FIVE

Personal Application

Application from Day One

Abraham took an oath at the well in Beersheba. The king asked Abraham to swear that he would never again deal falsely with him or his descendants. As we discovered in our lesson, after taking this oath, there is no record of Abraham being deceptive with anyone again.

To refresh your memory, look back at Abraham's words to Abimelek recorded in Genesis 20:13. What lie had Abraham asked his wife to tell everywhere they went?

Abraham took the oath as Abimelek requested. In fact, it was more than simply a promise to be honest in the future; Abraham made a blood covenant with Abimelek, and, as the two men walked between the pieces of the slaughtered animals, they were agreeing before God that the Lord would treat them like those slain animals if they violated the terms of the covenant (Jeremiah 34:18).

Making a vow to God is serious business. Read Ecclesiastes 5:4-5 and note what you learn about making a vow before God:

_____

Read what Jesus had to say on this topic in His famous Sermon on the Mount (Matthew 5:33-37). What is your conclusion about whether Christians should make vows to God?

_____

_____

Although Abraham's commitment to honesty appears to have greatly impacted him, we would do best to avoid making vows and simply say "Yes" or "No" in agreements. Let's ask God to help us stay honest through the power of His Spirit living within us as believers in Jesus, but let's avoid making rash promises to God that we may not be able to keep.

Application from Day Two

As Abraham stood atop a mountain in Moriah and prepared to offer Isaac as a sacrifice, he "reasoned that God could even raise the dead," and so he just chose to trust God during this revelatory test of his faith.

What does 1 John 3:20 tell us about God?

_____

Our Lord already knew Abraham would pass his test that day. Therefore, what is the logical conclusion regarding the purpose of Abraham's test?

_____

_____

Read Psalm 66:10 and James 1:3. What do you learn about some of the reasons God tests us?

> Was there ever a time when you had to act upon your faith, trusting God to handle the outcome?

Was there ever a time when you had to act upon your faith, trusting God to handle the outcome when obedience to His Word might have yielded some unpleasant results? How did that test refine you, help you to develop perseverance, or provide you with a greater understanding of God or yourself?

_____

_____

_____

Abraham's test revealed the depth of his faith *in* God and the results revealed the faithfulness *of* God. Tests are never pleasant, but it seems we humans learn best when lessons are taught on the altar of potential suffering or heartache.

Application from Day Three

When the angel of the Lord called to Abraham as he stood over Isaac with knife drawn, the Patriarch responded, "Here I am." To refresh your memory, re-read Hebrews 10:5-7 and note how Jesus responded when it was time for Him to come to earth as the atoning sacrifice and Savior of the world:

> How will you respond when God calls you to serve Him?

_____

How will you respond when God calls you to serve Him? Will you say, "Here I am . . . I have come to do Your will"? Will you be willing to serve God if to do so may involve pain or suffering or loss? Would you be willing to give up your rights or your comfort to answer God's call to serve Him? Write your thoughts below:

_____

_____

> God often calls us to serve Him by making us aware of something that needs to be done.

God often calls us to serve Him by making us aware of something that needs to be done. Do you know anyone in your neighborhood who has an unmet need right now? Does your church need volunteers somewhere on Sunday mornings? Take a moment to pray and ask God to show you how He wants you to serve Him right now. Ask Him to make you aware of something that needs to be done, and then answer His call to serve with the words, "Here I am. I have come to do Your will." If you are doing this study with a group, be prepared to share how you met a need this week.

Application from Day Four

God is the divine orchestrator. He is always at work (John 5:17), and we can rest assured He is crafting something "good and beautiful" through our lives when we choose to "love Him and accept His invitation to live according to His plan" (Romans 8:28 VOICE). Our awareness of God's activity and His faithfulness is what enables us to develop an unwavering faith in our God.

There is nothing like a personal testimony to strengthen someone's faith in God. On the lines below, write a short testimony of God's activity in your life. This can be something as profound as your salvation experience, or your testimony can be as simple as the means by which God brought you

> There is nothing like a personal testimony to strengthen someone's faith in God.

to your current city or church. The key is to highlight how you recognized God's activity through your circumstances and/or the positive changes that took place as a result of His work. If you are doing this study with a group, share your testimonies at your next meeting. If you are doing this study on your own, share your testimony with a friend or co-worker. Then watch God use your testimony to strengthen your listener(s) faith.

WEEK SIX

_____

_____

_____

_____

_____

_____

_____

_____

Week 7
Significant Conclusions

Saying Goodbye

She died at Kiriath Arba (that is, Hebron) in the land of Canaan,
and Abraham went to mourn for Sarah and to weep over her.

GENESIS 23:2

I enjoy writing studies based upon the perspectives of men and women whose stories God chose to include in the Scriptures. Biblical characters help bring God's Word to life. They make the principles seem more relevant and show us how to (and not to) live out those principles in our everyday lives. Unfortunately, today's lesson is an example of the downside of this approach to Bible study. We have to say goodbye to men and women with whom we have formed a connection. Today, we watch as our big-hearted patriarch mourns the loss of his beloved wife and partner in God's call: Sarah.

> Today, we watch as our big-hearted patriarch mourns the loss of his beloved wife.

Begin today by reading Genesis 23:1-2.

If you have ever seen a man grieving the loss of his wife, you can picture the expression on Abraham's face as he mourned and wept over Sarah. Nothing impacts me more powerfully than the sight of a man weeping. Abraham was a strong, respected man. He lost his brother when he was still living in his hometown of Ur. He left behind his country, his people, and eventually dealt with the death of his father before arriving in Canaan. He sent his firstborn son away to live elsewhere and packed Ishmael and Hagar's meager provisions himself. Abraham bound his son of promise and prepared to lose him on that altar of sacrifice. But it is only at the death of his wife that Scripture records Abraham weeping.

> If you have ever seen a man grieving the loss of his wife, you can picture the expression on Abraham's face as he mourned and wept over Sarah.

What does Genesis 2:24 indicate happens between a husband and wife?

Abraham dearly loved Sarah. They had followed God's call together, experienced the birth of their son of promise together, and now, the Father of a Multitude had to figure out how to continue his journey with God without Sarah.

Please read Genesis 23:3-9.

After weeping and mourning, I would guess Abraham was just like many of us when we are trying to cope with something with which we are unprepared to handle. He needed something tangible upon which to focus his attention and efforts, and the first task was giving his beloved Sarah a proper burial.

According to verse 2, where was Sarah when she died?

Hebron is in the heart of the Promised Land. Interestingly, according to Genesis 13:18, where did Abraham and Sarah live after Lot had chosen to go and live in Sodom?

Abraham was familiar with the cave he was requesting in Hebron and he knew exactly who owned that property. When the Hittites agreed to let Abraham secure a location to bury his wife, he asked the people to talk to Ephron on his behalf. However, Abraham's Divine Orchestrator saw fit to place Ephron among those gathered there that day.

Let's see what Ephron had to say. Please read Genesis 23:10-16.

What had Abraham originally desired to purchase (vs. 9)? _____

What did Ephron offer to give Abraham (vs. 11)?

_____

What did Abraham insist upon doing in verse 13? _____

Ephron's offer to give the field and the cave may have been an attempt to maintain the rights and eventually have the option of taking the field and cave back from Abraham. His seemingly generous offer may actually have been rooted in selfishness. The *New American Commentary* notes:

"Extravagant language and behavior often accompany the haggle: friendliness and expressions of affections may give way to ridicule and oaths. In the Middle East, the buyer may be addressed with kinship language and offered the item as a 'gift.' However, haggling is usually perceived as a practice that is socially negative. . . If so, Ephron's behavior is not benevolent but self-serving."[36]

In this exchange, Abraham insisted he pay the "price of the field." No haggling. No gifts. Right there in front of all the people gathered at the gate of Hebron, Abraham weighed out the four hundred shekels of silver, which weighed about 12 grams.[37] In today's value, that would be a little over $2,000.00.[38] Not a high price, but evidently a fair price.

Please read Genesis 23:17-20.

Abraham now owned a well in Beersheba and a cave, field, and all of the trees within the borders of that field in Hebron. That cave did indeed turn out to be a burial site for Abraham's descendants for generations to come. It occurs to me that purchasing that field and burying Sarah's body there was another testimony to Abraham's unwavering faith in God. Had the Lord failed to one day give Abraham's descendants the land of Canaan as He promised, he and Sarah would have forever been buried on foreign soil.

How did Abraham describe himself in Genesis 23:4?

_____

Read Hebrews 11:11-16 from your Bible and then read verse 11 below:

WEEK SEVEN

And by faith even Sarah, who was past childbearing age, was enabled to bear children because she considered Him faithful who had made the promise (NIV).

What happened as a result of Abraham and Sarah's faith?

Now read Hebrews 11:13 below and underline what Sarah and Abraham (along with Abel, Enoch, and Noah) accepted and confessed:

All these I have mentioned died in faith without receiving the full promises, although they saw the fulfillment as though from a distance. These people accepted and confessed that they were strangers and foreigners on this earth (VOICE).

Abraham and Sarah were not only strangers and foreigners in Canaan; they accepted that, as followers of God, they were strangers and foreigners on this earth. They were looking forward to the heavenly home God was preparing for them (Hebrews 11:16).

> Like Abraham, as believers in Jesus, we can look forward to a better country—a heavenly one—being prepared for us.

Like Abraham, as believers in Jesus, we can look forward to a better country—a heavenly one—being prepared for us. Abraham had to say goodbye to his beloved Sarah and continue to follow God and live out the rest of his days without her. But by faith, he could look forward to seeing Sarah again in that heavenly place.

Saying goodbye when someone we love dies is indescribably painful. Although grief manifests itself in many different ways, the loss often impacts us for the rest of our time on this earth. What encouragement does 1 Thessalonians 4:13-18 offer someone after the loss of a loved one?

To close our lesson today, let's take a peek at that heavenly place that awaits us. Please read Revelation 21:1-4.

He who overcomes [the world by adhering faithfully to Christ Jesus as Lord and Savior] will inherit these things, and I will be his God and he will be My son. (Revelation 21:7 AMP)

WEEK SEVEN   DAY TWO

Sarah and Hagar

*It is for freedom that Christ has set us free. Stand firm, then,
and do not let yourselves be burdened again by a yoke of slavery.*

GALATIANS 5:1

*I*n our Day One lesson, Abraham wept over the loss of his beloved Sarah and secured a burial site for her body in the heart of the Promised Land. As is appropriate at the burial of a man's wife, the ceremony and details that took place at that cave of Machpelah in Hebron remain a private matter between Abraham's family and His God. No details of Sarah's funeral are given at the end of Genesis 23. No attendees are listed. No eulogy is recorded. However, in today's lesson, we will create our own eulogy for Sarah by reviewing what Scripture records as an allegorical meaning for Sarah's role as the mother of Isaac, the child of God's covenantal promise.

The context for today's lesson is a gathering of a church in Galatia during the first century following the death of Christ. Although the members in attendance were believers in Jesus, there was a group of influential Messianic Jews (Jews who had accepted Jesus as Messiah and Savior) among them who were teaching the Gentile Christians that, in addition to their faith in Jesus, they needed to adhere to the Jewish laws, celebrate the festivals, and get circumcised in order to be accepted by God. The apostle Paul was concerned for the people in Galatia, many of whom Paul had probably led to faith in Christ. He penned a letter to the churches in Galatia and used Sarah as an illustration to help them understand the truth that, as believers in Jesus, we are free from the burdens of the Jewish law. So as we read a part of his letter, I encourage you to get comfortable. Pour a fresh cup of coffee, if it will help you concentrate, and let's see how Sarah's memory is honored through this eulogy of sorts, written by the Apostle Paul for the churches in Galatia, which is also deeply meaningful and applicable for you and for me.

Begin by reading Galatians 4:21-28 and fill in the missing information in the chart below to organize the details provided about Sarah and Hagar.

WEEK SEVEN

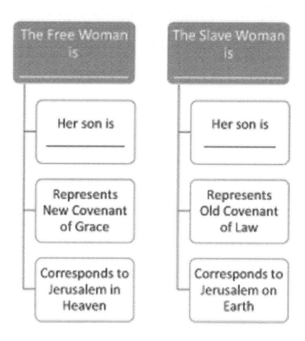

Let's focus first on Hagar. In Paul's illustration, she represents the Old Covenant, which is the law outlined in the first five books of our Bibles. The law was represented by the Ten Commandments God gave to the people through Moses on Mount Sinai.

Now read Galatians 3:23-25 and note how Paul described the law in verse 24:

_____

The law was put in place as a guardian or tutor, as the King James Version interprets it. As we discussed before, the law taught the people God's expectations, His purposes, and His ways; it was the means of setting boundaries and expectations for God's people.

Read Romans 3:20 and state the purpose of the law in your own words below:

_____

Hagar was a slave woman. She represented the city of Jerusalem where the temple sacrifices were performed, which only temporarily covered sins but could never remove them. She represented the law, as we discussed before—a guardian and tutor to make the people aware of their sin.

> The law was put in place as a guardian. God sent His Son, Jesus, to redeem those under the law (Galatians 4:4-5), and He accomplished what the law never could.

Paul made another important distinction between Sarah and Hagar related to the births of Abraham's sons. Fill in the blanks below from Galatians 4:23:

Ishmael was _____.

Isaac was _____.

The NIV says Ishmael was born according to "the flesh." When the word, "flesh" is used in the Bible, it is referring to our natural, sinful natures. From what you have learned in this study about the births of these two sons, what do you think Paul had in mind as he made this distinction?

_____

_____

Ishmael was the result of Abraham and Sarah's attempt to make God's promise a reality through their own methods. Similarly, Christians in Galatia were attempting to earn the Lord's favor and blessing through their efforts to keep the law. We cannot make God's plans come to pass using the world's philosophies and cultural customs. Likewise, despite our greatest efforts, we are unable to save ourselves by keeping the letter of the law.

In contrast, Isaac was brought about by divine intervention. God alone made the impossible a reality when Sarah—a woman who had been barren her entire life and was well beyond childbearing years—gave birth to Abraham's son of promise. Likewise, when the time was right, God sent His Son, Jesus, to redeem those under the law (Galatians 4:4-5), and He accomplished what the law never could, when Jesus gave His life as the atoning sacrifice for all sin for all time. Our sins were not only covered; they were removed (Hebrews 9:26). Through the power of His Spirit, God raised Jesus from the dead and sent His Spirit to live in the hearts of all who believe. Furthermore, when we accept Jesus as our Savior, we receive the promise of eternal life with our Lord in Heaven (1 John 2:25). We did not deserve any of it. It is a free gift from our loving God. That is why the New Covenant is called the Covenant of Grace.

It is by grace though faith in Jesus that we are saved (Ephesians 2:8), and Sarah represented the New Covenant established by God through Jesus.

How are believers in Christ described in Galatians 4:28?

_____

WEEK SEVEN

Sarah gave birth to Isaac, the one through whom the promised Seed of Abraham—Jesus—would come. She represents the New Covenant and the heavenly Jerusalem.

How is that heavenly city described in Hebrews 12:22?

> Sarah represents the New Covenant and the heavenly Jerusalem.

See, through Christ Jesus, the law of the Spirit who gives life has set us free from the law of sin and death (Romans 8:2). When we choose to belong to Christ, we become Abraham's seed and heirs according to the promise (Galatians 3:29). We, like Isaac, are children of the promise. We are not children of the slave woman, but of the free woman (Galatians 4:31).

We are free from the burdens of the Jewish law. We cannot find salvation through our own efforts and we will never be good enough to earn God's favor. Remember Sarah whenever you fall into the trap of trying to earn your salvation by keeping the letter of the law. It is for freedom that Christ has set us free. Paul wanted the Galatians (and us!) to understand that Sarah's legacy is freedom through Christ. Now that is what I call a eulogy.

WEEK SEVEN DAY THREE

In Search of a Wife

The LORD God said, "It is not good for the man to be alone.
I will make a helper suitable for him."

GENESIS 2:18

S arah was buried in the cave of Machpelah, located in a field in Hebron that was deeded to Abraham as his first official piece of the Promised Land. Isaac was about thirty-seven when his mother died, making Abraham somewhere around the age of a hundred and thirty-seven. As we begin chapter 24 in Genesis, Abraham has begun a new chapter of his life. Peek ahead for a moment.

What does Genesis 25:1 tell us Abraham did after Sarah's death?

_____

I think of God's words to Adam back in the Garden of Eden. According to Genesis 2:18, what did God say to Adam before He created Eve?

_____

Abraham apparently concurred. In fact, he evidently was concerned about Isaac's lack of a helpmate to support and accompany him on his own journey with God. Not to mention, Isaac was the son through whom Abraham's offspring would become as numerous as the stars in the sky. He was the son through whom God would keep His promises. Isaac also needed a wife.

Please read Genesis 24:1-4.

From where did Abraham ask his servant to get a wife for Isaac?

_____

WEEK SEVEN

Although God gave these instructions to His people many years later, Deuteronomy 7:1-4 provides a little insight into the reasons Abraham insisted Isaac's wife come from among his relatives. What did God indicate would happen if Abraham's descendants intermarried with the Canaanite people?

_____

Let's continue eavesdropping on Abraham's conversation with his servant. Please read Genesis 24:5-9.

What logical question did the servant ask Abraham in verse 5?

_____

The servant certainly could not force a woman to return with him to Canaan. You can almost sense panic in Abraham's response to his servant's question when he said, "Make sure that you do not take my son back there." Abraham did not know who the wife would be, but one thing was certain: Isaac was not to go back to live in Mesopotamia. He and his descendants were to live in the Promised Land.

How does Abraham's explanation in verse 7 reflect his unwavering faith that God would do whatever was necessary to fulfill His promises?

_____

God keeps His Word. Abraham had faith that "the Lord, the God of heaven" who brought him out of Ur and made a one-sided covenant, guaranteeing his offspring would receive the land of Canaan, would be faithful to provide a young woman from among his relatives who was willing to also leave _her_ country, _her_ people, and _her_ father's household to become Isaac's wife and participate in the fulfillment of God's promise.

Abraham's servant swore to get a wife from among his relatives back in Mesopotamia. Let's see what happened as he set out on this journey. Please read Genesis 24:10-21.

How did the servant ask God to confirm which young woman was His choice to be the wife of Abraham's son, Isaac (vs. 14)?

_____

According to verse 10, how many camels did the servant have with him? _____

"A thirsty camel can drink up to thirty gallons of water in about thirteen minutes."[39] Approximately how many gallons of water does that mean Rebekah probably drew from the well to provide enough water for those ten camels?

Let's just say she made a lot of trips back and forth to that well as Abraham's servant watched her closely to determine whether she was indeed Isaac's future wife. When she finished drawing and pouring . . . and drawing and pouring . . . all of that water, I do not see how there could be any doubt that she was the one for Isaac. But Abraham's servant was not finished with his seemingly imposing requests of this young, astoundingly gracious woman. Please read Genesis 24:22-28.

I am amazed at the hospitality Rebekah offered this stranger with ten thirsty camels. Actually, from his immediate response of bowing down to worship God right there in front of Rebekah, I think the servant was a bit overwhelmed himself. He had prayed for such an unrealistic, specific scenario that I wonder whether he ever really expected to find a young woman who would make such an offer to a stranger and then be willing to leave her homeland to come back and be Isaac's bride.

> I am amazed at the hospitality Rebekah offered this stranger with ten thirsty camels.

Abraham had become a man of unwavering faith. One thing I have noticed about people who possess great faith and wait with expectation for the Lord to do something amazing in order to accomplish His purposes in their lives: they are often met with skepticism from those with far less faith.

According to Matthew 17:20, what did Jesus say about the way God responds to a person who possesses even as little faith as might be compared to a tiny mustard seed?

Faith is the evidence of things not yet seen (Hebrews 11:1). Faith says God will do whatever is necessary to accomplish His will. If a mountain needs to move for God's purposes to prevail, then when one of His children asks Him to move it and trusts Him to do it, even the impossible can happen. Abraham and Sarah had experienced God overcoming the impossible when Sarah gave birth to Isaac at the ripe old age of ninety. Abraham knew God would provide a wife

> Faith says God will do whatever is necessary to accomplish His will.

WEEK SEVEN

for Isaac from among His relatives because that is what was necessary for His promised lineage to continue.

Abraham's servant was so overwhelmed when God did what he obviously thought would be impossible, the emotional man bowed down and worshipped and praised God right there in front of Rebekah. What did he specifically praise God for doing, according to verse 27?

The word translated as "kindness" in the NIV is once again the Hebrew word *hesed*. The servant praised God for treating Abraham with covenant kindness, for remaining loyal to His covenant purposes in Abraham's life.

As Rebekah heard the servant's praises, I would guess she was overwhelmed to discover this stranger whom she had graciously served and invited to her home was the servant of her relative Abraham. According to verse 28, what did Rebekah immediately do without waiting for the man to follow her back home?

God moved a mountain, so to speak, when He inspired Rebekah to serve a stranger with ten thirsty camels without complaint or hesitation. He boosted the faith of Abraham's servant when He provided the exact scenarios the skeptical servant had requested to identify Isaac's future bride. Tomorrow, we will watch as the Lord moves another mountain or two in order to bring Isaac the wife through whom He would continue to fulfill His covenant promise. Indeed, it was not God's will for Isaac to be alone.

WEEK SEVEN · DAY FOUR

She Said "Yes"

So they called Rebekah and asked her,
"Will you go with this man?" "I will go," she said.

GENESIS 24:58

Abraham's servant, probably named Eliezer (Genesis 15:2), found God's choice of a wife for Isaac among his master's relatives. Only God could have arranged for the granddaughter of Abraham's brother, Nahor, (Look back at the chart on page 117) to visit the well at the precise time Eliezer arrived. As if that were not already amazing enough, God inspired Rebekah to give Eliezer a drink, water all ten of his thirsty camels, and even invite him (and his camels!) to stay the night with her family.

Upon discovering this man was the servant of her long lost relative, Abraham, and being presented with the gold nose ring and bracelets, Rebekah was so flustered she forgot to wait for Eliezer to accompany her back to her house.

Let's see what happened next. Please read Genesis 24:28-38.

Who went back to the spring to get Eliezer? _____

After the camels were unloaded and fed and the men washed their feet, Rebekah's hospitable family prepared a meal for Eliezer and his men. How did Eliezer respond (vs.33)?

_____

Eliezer immediately began to explain his mission. Read Genesis 24:39-41. What did he feel was important for Rebekah's family to know as he began to explain his purpose?

_____

WEEK SEVEN

Eliezer, in essence, gave the family permission to say "no" to the wedding proposal he was about to offer. His master, Abraham, had faith God would send His angel to make the mission a success. However, just in case the family did not want to give Rebekah's hand in marriage to Isaac, Eliezer wanted them to know he would be released from his obligation to the oath he made to Abraham.

Let's see how Eliezer handled the rest of this marriage proposal. Please continue reading Genesis 34:42-49.

According to verse 49, how did Eliezer finish his proposal?

Eliezer's wording reminded me of those notes boys would pass to cute girls back in my elementary school days with the scribbled words "Do you like me, yes or no?" Eliezer was following his master's instructions to the letter, but he gave Laban and Rebekah's family every opportunity to turn down the offer. One thing was certain: Eliezer would have no doubt Rebekah was God's choice, if this marriage proposal ended in success.

Continue reading Genesis 24:50-51. How did Rebekah's brother and father respond?

Despite every sign Eliezer had requested and our Divine Orchestrator had granted, Abraham's servant still appeared to doubt whether Abraham's unwavering faith had been rewarded. Yet, as the details of Eliezer's journey and meeting with Rebekah were shared, two men who most likely worshipped other gods (Joshua 24:2) clearly recognized this meeting at that spring was "from the Lord." The men were so convinced they did not want to even say a word. They did not want to interfere in the abundantly clear move of Abraham's God. They immediately instructed Eliezer to take Rebekah back to be Isaac's wife.

Let's see what happened next. Please read Genesis 24:52-54.

What did Eliezer give to Rebekah and her family?

In that culture, "at the time of the betrothal, gifts of jewelry (which were often made of gold set with semiprecious stones) would be presented to the girl and sometimes to her mother, and . . . often the bride-price, dowry, or contract would also be exchanged."[40]

The bride-price was an amount paid by the groom's family to the family of the bride as a form of compensation when she moved to another family. A dowry was an amount given to the bride's father, which was kept in trust for the wife in case she was ever widowed or divorced; it also can refer to the amount a bride brought into the marriage.[41]

We are not told what negotiations might have taken place, but it is apparent Eliezer was quite generous to Rebekah and her family. With his mission accomplished, Eliezer and his men enjoyed a nice dinner with Abraham's relatives and went to bed. I believe Eliezer's faith was increased that day. He had asked for so many specific signs to confirm the identity of Isaac's future bride and provided two different opportunities for the family to deny his request; yet, this was so clearly a move of God that even Rebekah's family acknowledged it. However, the next morning, Rebekah's family hesitated. They wanted her to stay with them for a few more days. Let's see how Eliezer responded.

Please read Genesis 24:54-61.

What might Eliezer's response in verse 56 indicate about his faith at that point in his journey?

_____

When Rebekah said she was ready to immediately leave with Eliezer, what two blessings did her family speak over her, according to verse 60?

1). May you increase _____

2). May your offspring _____

In the culture of that time, when a man expressed a blessing over someone, it was a wish or prayer for a blessing that is to come in the future.[42] I would say this blessing was also a bit prophetic.

Look back at Genesis 22:17. What similar wording did God use as He confirmed His covenant blessings to Abraham after he was willing to sacrifice Isaac at Moriah?

_____

God indeed planned to show His goodness and kindness to Rebekah and Isaac and fulfill the promises He made to Abraham through the couple's offspring. They would continue the family line that would ultimately become as numerous as the stars in the sky.

WEEK SEVEN

Many years later, under the leadership of Joshua, Isaac and Rebekah's descendants would one day possess the cities of their enemies when they conquered the Canaanites and took possession of the Promised Land.

Let's see what happened as Rebekah left with Eliezer, ironically, riding one of those thirsty camels she watered at their first meeting.

Please read Genesis 24:61-67.

Where were Isaac and Rebekah married (vs. 67)?

> God indeed planned to show His goodness and kindness to Rebekah and Isaac and fulfill the promises He made to Abraham through the couple's offspring.

According to Genesis 25:20, how old was Isaac when he married Rebekah?

As a mother of a son, I find it quite endearing that Isaac was obviously still grieving the loss of his mother three years after her death. I am also touched that Scripture confirms Isaac loved Rebekah. She was not just the wife of an arranged marriage. She was not just a woman who met Abraham's criteria. She was a wife whose husband loved her enough that her presence and companionship helped him get over the loss of his mother. Rebekah heard her father and brother confirm that Eliezer's mission to find her had been "from the Lord." She left her family knowing very little about Isaac, but she experienced God's goodness and kindness through the love of her husband after she chose, by faith, to say "yes" to Eliezer's God-orchestrated marriage proposal.

WEEK SEVEN | DAY FIVE

Personal Application

Application from Day One

In Day One we watched as Abraham said goodbye to his wife of many long and eventful years. Both Abraham and Sarah had grown to become men and women of unwavering faith, and to honor Sarah's life, we used a portion of the Apostle Paul's letter to the Christians in Galatia as a eulogy.

Someday, your family members and friends are going to gather together to pay tribute to your life. If that were to happen today, what do you think would be said about your faith in God? Would your co-workers be surprised to discover you were a Christian? Do you think there would be people present who would say your faith in God impacted their lives? Would a story be told of how you trusted God despite the challenges or disappointments along your journey?

If you could determine what would be said about your life and your legacy, what would you want people to say?

> Someday, your family members and friends are going to gather together to pay tribute to your life.

> As long as you still have breath in your lungs, you have time to impact your legacy.

As long as you still have breath in your lungs, you have time to impact your legacy. Spend a few moments in prayer and ask God to show you what you need to do from this day forward in order to make that eulogy a reality.

Application from Day Two

As a believer in Jesus, you are a child of the free woman, Sarah (Galatians 4:31). You, like Isaac, are a child of the promise. You are Abraham's seed, and [an heir] according to the promise (Galatians 3:29).

As heirs, we have the same power that raised Jesus from the dead within us (Romans 8:11). We can call God Father because as believers in Jesus, we have been adopted and we are His children (Romans 8:15). We can be led and empowered by the Spirit of God. However, we can also resist the Spirit and quench the Spirit (1 Thessalonians 5:19), and we can live in defeat like we are children of the slave woman, Hagar, rather than the free woman, Sarah.

Look back at the eulogy you wrote on the lines above. I do not have to know specifics to know you need the power of the Spirit of the Living God guiding you in order to make that a reality.

Let's draw some additional application from Paul's letter to the Galatians. Read Galatians 5:13-26 for a description of what it means to live by the Spirit versus living by the flesh. This is not a list of ways you earn your salvation or become "good enough" to earn God's favor. These passages simply provide a contrast between the actions of people who live like slaves to their sinful nature and those who choose to live in the power of God's Spirit.

What are some of the contrasts outlined in these passages?

Living According to the Flesh: _____

_____

Living According to the Spirit: _____

_____

Take a few moments to consider where you may be yielding to your flesh nature rather than being sensitive to God's Spirit. What is one flesh-oriented behavior that you believe may be undermining the legacy you want to leave behind when your time on this earth is over?

_____

Pray right now for a greater sensitivity to God's Spirit with regard to that behavior.

Application from Days Three and Four

In our Day Three lesson, Abraham sent his servant, Eliezer, to get a wife for Isaac from Mesopotamia. Okay, ladies, if you are married, this application may step on your spiritual toes a bit. We will continue the theme of focusing on developing our legacies. Look again at the words God said to Adam back in the Garden of Eden, just before He created the very first wife, Eve.

According to Genesis 2:18, what did God say he would make for Adam?

_____

There is no greater legacy a married woman can leave behind than for people to remember her as a woman who lovingly supported her husband through all of life's ups and downs. Many of you took a traditional vow before God, promising "to have and to hold [your husband]" from your wedding day forward, for better, for worse, for richer, for poorer, in sickness and in health. You promised to love and to cherish him until death do you part. God desires for every husband and wife to take that vow seriously and commit to live out those vows in their marriage relationship. However, people rarely tell you, that in order to do that, you both need to be living in the power of the Holy Spirit.

A man needs his wife to respect him and support him in all of his endeavors. That does not mean we cannot express our opinions in a respectful, loving, and (from my experience) well-timed manner.

> A man needs his wife to respect him and support him in all of his endeavors.

If you are not married, just consider this lesson to be food for thought. If you are divorced, this lesson is not at all intended to make you feel sad or condemned. I have talked to so many women who have gone through the heartache and grief of a failed relationship. Please remember, just as Hagar was assured when she was alone in the desert, our God hears and is aware of all the misery you experienced.

But if you are currently married, please take a moment and ask God to reveal one way you can better support and help your husband in the stage of his life right now. After praying, write your thoughts below:

_____

_____

_____

Consider applying this lesson by taking the time to tell your husband something he has done for which you are grateful and appreciative. Be specific. Give examples. Sometimes our words of affirmation and appreciation are our greatest method of showing our support and love to our husbands. Write a note, talk to him face to face, or send a series of encouraging short texts to him throughout the week. Ask God to provide the opportunity and show you the right timing. He designed you as well as your husband. He knows just how you can be a greater help and support to your husband.

Love does not delight in evil but rejoices with the truth. It always protects, always trusts, always hopes, always perseveres. Love never fails . . . (1 Corinthians 13:6-8a)

If you are currently married, please take a moment and ask God to reveal one way you can better support and help your husband. Consider applying this lesson by taking the time to tell your husband something he has done for which you are grateful.

Week 8

Blessed to Bless

Honoring God's Friend

And the scripture was fulfilled that says, "Abraham believed God,
and it was credited to him as righteousness,' and he was called God's friend."

JAMES 2:23

Last week we said goodbye to Abraham's beloved wife Sarah. Today, as we begin to wrap up this eight-week study, we come to the end of Abraham's time here on earth. We will witness the end of an era, as the man who was an eyewitness to the promise breathes his last breath. Before we get to that, let's consider the events that occurred in Abraham's life after Sarah's death.

According to Genesis 25:1, what was the name of Abraham's new wife?

_____

How does 1 Chronicles 1:32 describe her? _____

According to the *New International Bible Dictionary*, concubines "enjoyed no other right but lawful cohabitation. They had no authority in the family or in household affairs. Their children were regarded as legitimate, although the children of the first wife were preferred in the distribution of the inheritance. The children of a concubine could, by means of small presents, be excluded from the heritage."[43]

Please read Genesis 25:1-7.

What were the names of Abraham's and Keturah's six sons (vs. 2)?

1) _____ 2) _____ 3) _____

4) _____ 5) _____ 6) _____

To whom did Abraham leave everything he owned?

_____

According to verse 6, what did Abraham give to Keturah's six sons?

_____

What conclusion can you make about the inheritance of Keturah's six sons, and how do you think their separation from Isaac may have protected the covenant promises God made to the Patriarch and his seed, Isaac?

_____

_____

_____

Once again, Abraham had to say goodbye to sons he surely loved, in order to protect the lineage of his son of the promise. He gave his six sons gifts and sent them to live outside of the Promised Land. According to verse 6, where did the sons of Keturah settle?

_____

While we are on the topic of Abraham's sons with his concubines, let's see what Scripture says about the descendants of Ishmael. Please read Genesis 25:12-18.

How many sons did Ishmael have (vs. 13-15)? _____

Where did they settle and with whom did they live in hostility (vs. 18)?

_____

_____

When Sarah began her creative family planning, she had no idea her scheme to create a son through Hagar would one day create an entire nation of people who would live in hostility toward the descendants of her promised son. When we attempt to make God's plans come to pass our way, we can expect consequences. Sadly, the region is filled with hostility to this day.

Ishmael and the six sons of Keturah were all sent to live in locations outside the territory of the Promised Land. Let's turn our focus now to the promised son, Isaac, and his family. Please read Genesis 25:19-26.

What were the names of Isaac's two sons?

_____ and _____

How old was Isaac when they were born (vs. 26)? _____

Abraham was about a hundred years old when he and Sarah had Isaac. Therefore, approximately how old was Abraham when Isaac's children were born?

_____

_____

I imagine Grandpa Abraham enjoyed spending what time he could with his grandchildren during the last fifteen years of his life. After spending eighty-six years as an Exalted Father with no children (Genesis 16:16), watching his family grow must have brought the Patriarch great joy.

How are his two grandsons described (vs. 25-26)?

Esau: _____

Jacob: _____

What insight into their unique temperaments do you gain from Genesis 25:28?

_____

_____

It always amazes me how children can share the same gene pool, grow up in the same household, and have many of the same life experiences, yet still look and behave so differently. Mark and I have two children. Our son, Brandon, walks like Mark, has mannerisms that remind me of Mark, yet his bone structure is smaller, like mine, and he is an introvert by nature, as I am. Brianna, on the other hand, has my eyes, my smile, and a similar frame to mine, but she is an extrovert, like her daddy. Brandon is a neatnik and thinks deeply about his circumstances before acting. In contrast, Bri lives life like a tornado, moving from task to task to task, with a natural tendency to leave a trail behind her. Their differences have caused conflicts between them over the years, but their unique personalities make me smile. I truly enjoy being their mother.

I suspect Abraham enjoyed being the grandfather of those twin boys. Hairy little Esau was apparently the apple of Isaac's eye, and his twin brother, Jacob, was probably what bullies today might have called a mamma's boy. The two sons were as opposite as brothers could be. I would guess Abraham spent as much time as he could with Esau and Jacob and explained the importance of obeying and following the Lord. He probably told them about life back in the city of Ur and made sure they understood that faith in God is worth far more than all the wealth and conveniences he left behind in Mesopotamia. I picture the boys sitting wide-eyed on their grandfather's lap—one on each knee—as he told them about the time God empowered his army to rescue their cousin Lot when he was captured by five powerful kings from the northern territories of Canaan. The Patriarch probably cautioned them about choosing their companions wisely when he told them about the destruction of the wicked cities of Sodom and Gomorrah. Perhaps the boys cheered as Grandpa Abe told them about the angels God sent to rescue Lot and his family, just before the skies rained down that burning sulfur. I trust Abraham told them of the miraculous birth of their father, Isaac, and of the covenant promises that were part of their heritage.

> Perhaps the boys cheered as Grandpa Abe told them about the angels God sent to rescue Lot and his family.

Read Genesis 25:7-11.

Where was Abraham buried? _____

Who buried him? _____

Apparently Ishmael returned from the region near Egypt to stand with his younger half-brother and say goodbye to their father. The Patriarch was buried alongside Sarah in that cave of Machpelah near Mamre—his first and only official piece of the Promised Land—land Abraham knew by faith God would one day grant to his descendants.

> The Lord had blessed Abraham in every way (Genesis 24:1).

The Lord had blessed Abraham in every way (Genesis 24:1). He had lived a full life. He had experienced loss, embraced change, and obediently followed his God through uncharted territories. He had been willing to sacrifice everything, including his son of promise, to obey his God. Abraham lived his life well. As he breathed his last breath, he had grown from an ordinary man living in his father's household and worshipping a god he believed controlled the moon, into a legendary man of unwavering faith in the true God of all the heavens and all the earth—a man who had the honor of being called God's friend (James 2:23).

WEEK EIGHT | DAY TWO

Promises Inherited

So in Christ Jesus you are all children of God through faith.

GALATIANS 3:26

Abraham lived a hundred and seventy-five years. He was an eyewitness to the promise and left this earth with the assurance that God's covenant blessings would be passed on to his descendants. Isaac was the first of those heirs. During the last years of Abraham's life, we can assume he had the privilege of spending time with Isaac's sons, Esau and Jacob. As the boys grew, their grandfather knew one of them would be the next heir to God's covenant promises.

If you recall, when Isaac's wife, Rebekah, was pregnant, God shared some specific information with her about her boys. Look back at Genesis 25:23.

> Abraham was an eyewitness to the promise and left this earth with the assurance that God's covenant blessings would be passed on to his descendants. Israel (Jacob) eventually married two women and he became the father of twelve sons.

Which son would serve the other? _____

Let's see what happened as the twins grew up. Please read Genesis 25:27-34.

What transpired between Esau and Jacob that began the fulfillment of the prophesy God spoke to Rebekah?

_____

_____

As the firstborn son, Esau stood to inherit his father's estate—both his physical possessions and his spiritual inheritance. Esau and Jacob spent about fifteen years around their grandfather. We can assume both young men were aware of God's covenant promises. Esau was the firstborn son. We do not know whether Rebekah shared God's prophecy with her favorite son, Jacob (vs.28), but it is apparent he recognized the value of the firstborn son's position in the family. Jacob wanted that birthright. Esau, on the other hand, was irreverent, impulsive, and seemingly unaffected by Abraham and Isaac's relationships with God or the significance of the covenant promises.

How is Esau described in Hebrews 12:16?

_____

Any parent should shudder at that description. Sadly, it is possible for a son raised in a family in which God is honored and worshipped to grow up to become a godless man. Esau did just that. If you have children (and/or nieces, nephews, or grandchildren), please write their names on the lines below. Then take a moment to pray for each child by name. Ask God to redeem all parenting mistakes. Ask Him to draw each child to Himself. Implore Him to use every experience they have (positive or negative) to mold them into the men and women they were designed to become when He knit them together in the womb (Psalm 139:13).

_____

_____

Interestingly, Jacob's name means "deceiver." He was a quiet, manipulative man who not only gained his brother's birthright, but, with the help of his mother, tricked his father, Isaac, into giving him the family blessing, as well. However, in contrast to Esau's godless state, Jacob eventually overcame his deceptive nature and developed his own relationship with the Lord of his grandfather Abraham and his father Isaac. In fact, just as God had changed Abram's name to Abraham and Sarai's name to Sarah in order to represent new seasons in their lives, God changed Jacob's name.

Read Genesis 35:9-13.

What was Jacob's new name? _____

What inheritance did God confirm would pass to Israel?

_____

Israel (Jacob) eventually married two women—sisters, in fact—named Leah and Rachel, and he became the father of twelve sons. Genesis 29:31 through 30:24 records the events that led to the births of eleven of those sons. Record their names below.

_____(29:32)   _____(30:11)

_____(29:33)   _____(30:13)

_____(29:34)   _____(30:18)

_____(29:35)   _____(30:20)

_____(30:6)   _____(30:24)

_____(30:8)   _____

Read Genesis 35:16-18 to find the name of the last son.

These sons were the physical descendants of Abraham and became known as the nation of Israel (or Israelites). They grew into a nation of people as numerous as the stars in the sky and eventually inhabited the Promised Land, just as God said they would.

Look back at Genesis 15:12-16. Note the events God told Abraham would occur before his descendants took possession of the land:

For four hundred years, the Israelites would _____

_____

Who would pass away prior to the Israelites taking possession of the land? _____

Read Joshua 21:43-45 and summarize the passages in your own words:

_____

WEEK EIGHT

The people of Israel are Abraham's physical descendants who later became known as the Jews. Gentiles (non-Jews) were excluded from a covenant relationship with our Lord until the promised Seed of Abraham, Jesus (Galatians 3:16), came to earth to reconcile us to God.

Read Ephesians 2:11-13.

Unless you are a Messianic Jew (a Jewish person who accepts Jesus as Messiah and Savior), you, like me, are considered a Gentile. According to verse 13, how are we, who were once alienated from God, brought near to Him?

_____

Now read Galatians 3:26-29 and summarize what Jesus did for us in your own words below:

_____

_____

Jew and Gentile alike have access to God the Father through faith in God the Son. As believers in Jesus, we are Abraham's children (seed) and heirs according the promise (Galatians 3:29). We have a beautiful eternal inheritance that awaits us in the city with foundations, whose architect and builder is our God (Hebrews 11:10) and our greatest inheritance is the promise of God Himself.

> Jew and Gentile alike have access to God the Father through faith in God the Son.

As we close today, write a prayer, thanking God for promises you have inherited because of Abraham's obedience to God's glorious plan:

_____

_____

_____

WEEK EIGHT · DAY THREE

Righteous by Faith

This righteousness is given through faith in Jesus Christ to all who believe.
There is no difference between Jew and Gentile.

ROMANS 3:22

When God told Abraham his descendants would one day be as numerous as the stars in the sky, Abraham chose to believe God, even though he could not reconcile any of the circumstances of his life with the reality God promised him. That is faith. As a result of his faith, God chose to declare Abraham righteous—in a position of right standing and innocent of all charges.

According to Romans 3:22-24, to whom is righteousness granted?

Is there a difference between the way Jews and Gentiles receive this status of righteousness before God?

Now read Romans 4:1-5. What is credited to us as righteousness?

We are saved by grace through faith in Jesus (Ephesians 2:8). If you recall from our Week Three lesson, to be considered righteous means that God—the ultimate Judge of all creation—declares us innocent of all charges against us. All have sinned and fall short of the glory of God (Romans 3:23), but all are justified freely by His grace through the redemption that came by Christ Jesus (Romans 3:24).

> We are saved by grace through faith in Jesus (Ephesians 2:8).

Abraham was considered righteous because he believed God's Word. He believed God's promises. He aspired to live a life of unwavering faith in his God, and that pursuit is what brought him righteousness. Abraham's life story should inspire us to also pursue a life of unwavering faith.

> Abraham was considered righteous because he believed God's promises.

Read Isaiah 51:1-3. (Mark your place, we will come back to these passages.)

Whose life do these passages invite us to examine, as confirmation that the pursuit of righteousness—a life of unwavering faith in our God—evokes God's blessing?

_____

According to verse 2, what blessing did God bring about in Abraham's life as a result of his unwavering faith?

_____

Abraham was a man with no children. His wife had been barren her entire life, and the couple was well beyond childbearing years. Abraham was simply living an ordinary life in Mesopotamia when God called him to leave his country, his people, and his father's household and go to a foreign land on faith.

Look at the description of Abraham in Hebrews 11:8-12. Of all Abraham's acts of faith, which one do you find most inspiring?

_____

_____

When God called Abraham, he was only one man. However, God blessed him because of his obedience and faith. He was as good as dead (Hebrews 11:12) because he had no descendants to live on after him. According to Genesis 15:2, who did Abraham originally assume would be his only heir?

Because of Abraham's unwavering faith in God, the Lord blessed him far beyond his wildest expectations. Today, his descendants, both physical and spiritual, are truly as numerous as the stars in the sky and as countless as the sand on the sea shores. He was truly blessed in every way (Genesis 24:1).

> Because of Abraham's unwavering faith in God, the Lord blessed him far beyond his wildest expectations.

As we aspire to also become people of unwavering faith, let's look a little more closely at Isaiah 51:1-3. Nestled into these passages are some of the blessings—expressions of God's kindness and goodness—we can anticipate as we pursue righteousness.

The Lord will surely comfort Zion . . . (Isaiah 51:3a)

We can anticipate the blessing of God's comfort.

As we pursue righteousness and aspire to live lives of unwavering faith, like Abraham, there will be times when we will make mistakes. As you reflect back on all you have learned about Abraham and Sarah, what mistakes can you remember from their journey with God?

WEEK EIGHT

Abraham made some pretty big blunders as he pursued a life of righteousness through faith. The most consequential error was agreeing to Sarah's plan to have a child through her maidservant, Hagar. The turmoil that decision created in Abraham's tents was probably a daily reminder of consequences that follow when people attempt to make God's will come to pass their own way.

> Abraham made some pretty big blunders as he pursued a life of righteousness through faith.

Yet, according to Genesis 17:1, how did God refer to Himself in His first recorded conversation with Abraham after the birth of Ishmael?

God Almighty. This name highlights the fact that God is all-powerful and all-sufficient. It means He is able to keep His promises. In other words, nothing is too hard for Him (Jeremiah 32:27), and He does not need our help to accomplish His purposes. God comforted Abraham by letting him know that He did not need Abraham or Sarah's help to make His promise come to pass. He is a mighty, powerful, and all-sufficient God.

Are there any mistakes you have made lately? Are you facing any obstacles or enduring some consequences? How does the fact that our God is all-powerful and all-sufficient comfort you personally today?

> Are there any mistakes you have made lately?

The Lord . . . will look with compassion on her ruins. (Isaiah 51:3a)

We can anticipate the blessing of God's compassion.

Look at the rest of God's words to Abraham from Genesis 17:2-4 below:

"I will prepare a contract between us, guaranteeing to make you into a mighty nation. In fact you shall be the father of not only one nation, but a multitude of nations!" Abram fell face downward in the dust as God talked with him (TLB).

What promise did God confirm He still intended to keep, despite the mistakes Abraham and Sarah had made along the way?

God made it clear to Abraham that in spite of all that had happened, He still intended to make him the father of many nations. How did Abraham respond to God's compassion?

I have been most overwhelmed by the compassion of our God when my actions have reflected a lack of faith and, yet, our gracious, compassionate God has still chosen to make his faithful presence and activity apparent in my life. A revelation of God's compassion often prompts heartfelt worship. Can you recall a time when you were overwhelmed by God's compassion for you? If so, what were the circumstances and how did you respond?

> Can you recall a time when you were overwhelmed by God's compassion for you?

Like Abraham, when we pursue life of unwavering faith in God, we will experience the blessing of God's comfort as He reminds us of His power to accomplish His plans and purposes for our lives. We will experience the blessing of His compassion as He mercifully continues to make His presence and activity evident to us, despite our mistakes and our weaknesses. Tomorrow, we will explore what Scripture tells us about the third blessing we can anticipate as we pursue a life of faith: the glorious blessing of transformation.

WEEK EIGHT

WEEK EIGHT | DAY FOUR

Transformative Faith

Therefore, if anyone is in Christ, he is a new creation;
the old has gone, the new has come!

2 CORINTHIANS 5:17 (NIV '84)

Yesterday, we focused our attention on Isaiah 51 and discovered that Abraham's life serves as an example for those of us who aspire to pursue righteousness—a life defined by unwavering faith in our God. When the Lord called Abraham, he was one man without any children, and because of his faith, God blessed him and made him the father of many nations. Along his journey, Abraham was comforted by the realization that God is all-powerful and all-sufficient; able to overcome any obstacle and always capable of keeping His promises. The Patriarch experienced the blessing of God's compassion when the Lord mercifully continued to carry out His plans for Abraham's life, despite all of his mistakes and weaknesses. Abraham lived a blessed life of faith. His blessings included God's comfort, His compassion, and, as we will reflect upon today, the remarkable blessing of a transformed life.

Let's begin today by reading the definition of faith as explained in Hebrews 11:1 from the Amplified Bible:

Now faith is the assurance (title deed, confirmation) of things hoped for (divinely guaranteed), and the evidence of things not seen [the conviction of their reality—faith comprehends as fact what cannot be experienced by the physical senses].

What evidence can you recall from Abraham's life that he comprehended as fact what he was unable to experience by his physical senses?

For the Patriarch, God's divine directive was all the assurance he needed to leave his country, his people, and his father's household. God's covenant promise was enough for him to live his life as a stranger and foreigner in Canaan, with steadfast confidence his descendants would one day possess that land. God had given His Word that the Child of Promise would come from his own body, and although Abraham made some poor decisions as he awaited the fulfillment of that promise, he chose to believe God and it was credited to him as righteousness.

Read Isaiah 51:1-3 again from your Bible.

. . . He will make her deserts like Eden, her wastelands like the garden of the LORD . . . . (Isaiah 51:3)

After Abraham and Sarah attempted to start a family through their maidservant, hostility, jealousy, and conflict took up residency within their tents.

Look back at Genesis 16:3-6.

After Hagar became pregnant, how did she feel toward her mistress, Sarai?

According to verse 6, how did Sarah treat Hagar? _____

Abraham was eighty-six years old when Ishmael was born. In Genesis 17:21, God told him his son of promise would finally arrive the following year. According to Genesis 17:1, how old was Abraham when that conversation took place?

Based upon the dynamics in their tents, I would guess those thirteen years after Ishmael was born were long, stressful years. Abraham and Sarah had tried to make God's will come to pass their own way. The hostility and jealousy that decision created strained all of their family relationships.

Once again, let's focus our attention on the conversation God had with Abraham as recorded in Genesis 17. Please read verses 1-8.

After making a mess of his household in pursuit of a son, Abraham was overcome with emotion as God reminded him to walk before Him *faithfully* and told him to be blameless (vs.1). The Patriarch fell on his face before God. He had not been faithful, and he certainly had not been blameless. Yet, God still chose to bless Abraham. The Lord reminded His Patriarch that He is all-sufficient and all-powerful. He confirmed His promises would still come to fruition. It was there, on his face before God, that Abram, "Exalted Father," became Abraham, "Father of Many." All of the stress and consequences had prepared him. Abraham was finally ready to become the father of many nations.

During that same conversation, God changed Sarai's name to Sarah. Interestingly, the New International Bible Dictionary lists the meaning of the name Sarai as "doubtful."[44] I have seen notes elsewhere indicating her original name meant "dominative." Can you think of some examples of times when the Matriarch's actions prior to the birth of Isaac reflected a dominative or doubtful nature?

Doubtful Sarai was renamed Sarah, which means "Princess."[45] Please read Genesis 17:15-16. What future events do you think her new name reflected?

When Abram and Sarai first started their journey with God, the designated Future-Patriarch had a natural tendency to lie when he faced uncertain circumstances. Sarai was dominative and doubtful. When the promised child had not arrived within her time-table, she took control, came up with her own plan to start a family, and ordered her husband to sleep with her maidservant. Passive Abram agreed to her plan without ever consulting God. Abram and Sarai had a lot of growing to do before they were ready to become Abraham and Sarah. However, when the time was right, God transformed their wastelands into gardens (Isaiah 51:3).

> Have you endured some consequences because of natural weaknesses?

Reflect upon your own journey with God. Have you endured some consequences because of natural weaknesses? Have you ever made ruins of a relationship? Can you recognize some struggles and consequences that increased your faith or prepared you to serve God in some way? Write your thoughts below:

_____

_____

_____

Read Isaiah 51:3 from an NIV Bible. Fill in the blanks below from verse 3:

. . . He will make her deserts like Eden, her wastelands like the garden of the Lord. _____*and* _____ *will be found in her, thanksgiving and the sound of singing.* (Isaiah 15:3b)

The greatest blessing we can anticipate when we pursue righteousness—a life of unwavering faith—is the glorious transformation that takes place in our hearts. An Abram becomes an Abraham. A Sarai becomes Sarah. By faith, a former liar and schemer becomes a man of integrity and the respected father of a nation; a previously doubtful and dominative wife becomes a gracious princess. By faith, a wasteland is transformed into a beautiful garden for God's glory. The old is gone, the new has come (2 Corinthians 5:17). When God blesses us by transforming a marriage, or breaking the chains of addiction, or carrying us through an unspeakable tragedy; when a lost and hurting soul finds healing in Christ; when we choose to trust God and comprehend His Word as fact, even when we cannot see evidence of His faithful presence with our five senses, that is when we discover that the greatest blessing of God is a transformed life. Joy and gladness well up within us. Thanksgiving springs forth from our lips, compelling us to sing praises to our Lord.

> The greatest blessing we can anticipate when we pursue righteousness is the glorious transformation that takes place in our hearts.

WEEK EIGHT

Blessed Faith

Now faith is the assurance (title deed, confirmation) of things hoped for (divinely guaranteed), and the evidence of things not seen [the conviction of their reality—faith comprehends as fact what cannot be experienced by the physical senses].

HEBREWS 11:1 AMP

I feel called to write Bible studies. In other words, just as God called Abraham to leave his country, his people, and his father's household to go to an unknown land on faith, I write because I feel compelled by the Spirit of God to do so. Even though I never quite know what a Bible study journey will entail, I always know I will be changed and stretched in the process. It seems my life's circumstances often parallel key lessons from each Bible study. When I wrote *Peter-Eyewitness to Majesty: Abandoning Self for Christ*, I was serving in my first church staff position where I learned to abandon my preconceived ideas about ministry work (which, I must say, were a bit naive) and embrace the reality that serving Christ requires far more sacrifice and humility than I ever imagined. When I was writing *Moses-Eyewitness to Glory: Discerning God's Active Presence*, I endured some devastating trials and felt more vulnerable than at any time in my life, before or since. I needed God and in my neediness He taught me to discern His active presence like never before. Writing about Abraham, this legendary man who developed unwavering faith, has been a faith-building journey for me personally. God has always been faithful in providing me with the time, energy, and lessons from His Word that were needed to complete each Bible study He has called me to write. However, along *this* journey I have had more unforeseen demands on my time and energy than I have ever had while writing. I have had family members with major illnesses who needed my help and support. I have had unexpected home repairs, a

> This study was written with a keen awareness of my dependence upon God.

vehicle stolen, and computer hardware issues. Each of my parents has been ill at different times, and unexpected needs have come up from my husband's business. I have forgone sleep and worked on lessons in both hotel rooms and doctors' waiting rooms. This study was written with a keen awareness of my dependence upon God. I have built some faith-muscles this year, and Abraham was my personal trainer.

What about you? As you have taken this journey with Abraham, has his story helped you build any faith-muscles? Have you had the opportunity to live out any of these lessons? If so, what have you learned?

_____

_____

_____

As we end this faith journey, it seems only fitting to return to the place where this man who developed an unwavering faith first began. Please read Genesis 12:1-3 one last time from your Bible. From memory, note some of the ways God made those promises a reality:

_____

_____

_____

Before we close our workbooks at the end of this lesson, I can think of a few pointers from Abraham's journey that we can take along with us as we aspire to develop unwavering faith.

Obey without fretting details.

Abraham left Ur without having any idea where he was going. He did not know how his family would grow food or find water for their livestock. He had no idea how he would provide for his family. Abraham just chose to follow God without trying to plan out all of the details.

Read what Jesus had to say about our tendency to worry, as recorded in Luke 12:22-31.

What faith-building truths did Jesus say we can glean from nature?

_____

Rather than physical needs, what should we seek as we aspire to obey God by faith (vs. 31)?

_____

Read and then re-write Hebrews 11:8 into a statement of how you should respond when God prompts you to make a change or to serve Him in some new role:

_____

_____

Wait without taking control.

Abraham and Sarah got tired of waiting for the child God promised them. Sarah took control and came up with an idea to start a family her own way. Abraham agreed to her plan without pausing to seek God's counsel. As it appeared time was running out for Abraham and Sarah to have a child, the couple wavered and attempted to get what they wanted their own way.

Often the greatest tests of our faith will come when we are waiting for God to change our circumstances or provide a perceived need. Read the passages below and note how each verse provides perspective during a time of waiting:

2 Peter 3:8-9: _____

Isaiah 40:12-14, 25-26: _____

Isaiah 55:8-11: _____

Read Lamentations 3:24 below from the Amplified Bible:

"The Lord is my portion and my inheritance," says my soul;
"Therefore I have hope in Him and wait expectantly for Him."

Waiting expectantly for God does not mean you should be idle or inactive. It means you refuse to force your own agenda or resort to dishonest, manipulative means to get what you want. God's will and God's ways are always in agreement with His Word. For example, if landing that great-paying job means you have to lie on a resume, it is not the job God has for you. Waiting expectantly for God means you will wait for a path that will honor Him and agrees with the principles in His Word. If you have more than

> Waiting expectantly for God does not mean you should be idle or inactive.

one option that honors God, pray and ask Him for the wisdom to choose the best path (James 1:5).

Write a prayer on the lines below, asking God to help you wait expectantly for Him without attempting to take control and force your own way:

_____

_____

_____

_____

Bless without counting the cost.

Abraham grew into a man of unwavering faith. Because he believed God is a promise-keeping God, all nations on earth have been blessed through him. God blessed Abraham and, indeed, the Patriarch fulfilled God's call to *be* a blessing (Genesis 12:2).

Be a blessing to others during your time on this earth. As a believer in Jesus, you are Abraham's seed and heirs to the promises of God. You have been blessed with unconditional love and merciful forgiveness. Bless others with the same. If God blesses you financially, prayerfully give generously to organizations and people who honor God with their work. Feed the poor, provide for widows and orphans. Be generous with your words, with your talents, with your time, and with your possessions. Aspire to live a life defined by unwavering faith in our God and then, *be* a blessing.

> Be a blessing to others during your time on this earth.

"And I will bless you [abundantly] . . .
And you shall be a blessing [a source of great good to others]."
(Genesis 12:2 AMP)

WEEK EIGHT

END NOTES

1. J. D. Douglas and Merrill C. Tenney, *New International Bible Dictionary*, (Grand Rapids, MI: Zondervan Publishing House, 1987), 7.
2. Ancient History Encyclopedia, http://www.ancient.eu/ur/ Web. 15, June, 2015
3. J. D. Douglas and Merrill C. Tenney, *New International Bible Dictionary*, (Grand Rapids, MI:Zondervan Publishing House, 1987), 167.
4. John F. Walvoord and Roy B Zuck, *The Bible Knowledge Commentary: Old Testament* (Colorado Springs, CO, Cook Communications Ministries, 2000), 47.
5. Lawrence O. Richards, *New International Encyclopedia of Bible Words*, (Grand Rapids, MI: Zondervan Publishing House, 1991), 375.
6. Ralph Gower, *The New Manners & Customs of Bible Times Student Edition*, (Chicago, IL : The Moody Bible Institute, 2000), 259.
7. John F. Walvoord and Roy B Zuck, *The Bible Knowledge Commentary: Old Testament* (Colorado Springs, CO : Cook Communications Ministries, 2000), 47.
8. *Webster's Unabridged Dictionary of the English Language*, (New York : Portland House, a division of Dilithium Press, Ltd, 1989), 827
9. William Whiston, *Josephus, The Complete Works* (Nashville, TN: Thomas Nelson Publishers, 1998), 44.
10. Kenneth A. Mathews, *The New American Commentary, Volume 1B* (Nashville, TN: B&H Publishing Group, 2005), 146.
11. John F. Walvoord and Roy B. Zuck, *The Bible Knowledge Commentary: Old Testament*, (Colorado Springs, CO : Cook Communications Ministries, 2000), 53.
12. Kenneth A. Mathews, *The New American Commentary, Volume 1B* (Nashville, TN: B&H Publishing Group, 2005), 153.
13. John McArthur, *The McArthur New Testament Commentary: Hebrews*, (Chicago, IL: Moody Publishers, 1983), 175.
14. *Webster's Unabridged Dictionary of the English Language*, (New York : Portland House, a division of Dilithium Press, 1989), 555.
15. C. F. Keil and F. Delitzsch, *Commentary on the Old Testament* (Peabody, MA: Hendrickson, 1996), Vol. 1, 138.
16. John F. Walvoord and Roy B. Zuck, *The Bible Knowledge Commentary: Old Testament*, (Colorado Springs, CO : Cook Communications Ministries, 2000), 56.
17. Ibid., 57.
18. Ibid., 58.
19. The Net Bible, (Biblical Studies Press, L.L.C. www.NETBIBLE.com, 2005) Study Notes 11, 41.
20. Lawrence O. Richards, *New International Encyclopedia of Bible Words,* (Grand Rapids, MI: Zondervan Publishing House, 1991), 566
21. John F. Walvoord and Roy B. Zuck, *The Bible Knowledge Commentary: New Testament*, (Colorado Springs, CO : Chariot Victor Publishing, 1983), 600.
22. Lawrence O. Richards, *New International Encyclopedia of Bible Words*, (Grand Rapids, MI: Zondervan Publishing House, 1991), 375.

23. Kenneth L. Barker and John R. Kohlenberger III, *The Expositor's Bible Commentary: Old Testament*, (Grand Rapids, MI: The Zondervan Corporation, 1994), 26.
24. John F. Walvoord and Roy B. Zuck, *The Bible Knowledge Commentary: Old Testament*, (Colorado Springs, CO : Cook Communications Ministries, 2000), 58.
25. Josephus, Translated by William Whiston, A.M., *Josephus: The Complete Works 1.11.4,* (Nashville, Tennessee : Thomas Nelson Publishers, 1998), 47.
26. Herbert Lockyer, *All the Women of the Bible*, (Grand Rapids, MI: Zondervan, 1967), 158.
27. *NIV Giant Print Reference Bible*, (Grand Rapids, MI: Zondervan, 2011), 28.
28. J. D. Douglas and Merrill C. Tenney, *New International Bible Dictionary*, (Grand Rapids, MI: Zondervan Publishing House, 1987), 665.
29. Barry J. Beitzel, *The Moody Atlas of Bible Lands*, (Chicago, IL: The Moody Bible Institute, 1985), 32.
30. John F. Walvoord and Roy B. Zuck, *The Bible Knowledge Commentary: Old Testament*, (Colorado Springs, CO : Cook Communications Ministries, 2000), 62.
31. Lawrence O. Richards, *New International Encyclopedia of Bible Words*, (Grand Rapids, MI: Zondervan Publishing House, 1991), 505.
32. *The New International Webster's Concise Dictionary of the English Language*, (Trident Press International, 1997), 824.
33. Kenneth A. Mathews, *The New American Commentary: Volume 1B, Genesis 11:27-50:26*, (B&H Publishing Group, 2005), 272.
34. Website Article. "Invaders of the Sonoran Desert Region, a Project of the Arizona Sonora-Desert Region Museum" http://www.desertmuseum.org/invaders/invaders_tamarisk.php, Web. 13, January, 2015.
35. W. E. Vine, Merrill F. Unger and William White, Jr., *Vine's Complete Expository Dictionary of Old and New Testament Words*, (Nashville, TN : Thomas Nelson, Inc., 1984, 1996), 10.
36. Kenneth A. Mathews, *The New American Commentary: Volume 1B*, (B&H Publishing Group, 2005), 320.
37. *The Holy Bible, New International Version* (Grand Rapids, MI : Biblica, Inc., published by Zondervan, 2011,), footnote k,1387.
38. http://www.silvergrambars.com/ January 23, 2016.
39. http://www.nationalgeographic.com/weepingcamel/thecamels.html January 25, 2016.
40. J. D. Douglas and Merrill C. Tenney, *New International Bible Dictionary*, (Grand Rapids, MI : Zondervan Publishing House, 1987), 1059.
41. Ralph Gower, *The New Manners & Customs of Bible Times; Student Edition*, (Chicago, IL : The Moody Bible Institute of Chicago, 2000), 48, 52.
42. W. E. Vine, Merrill F. Unger, William White Jr., *Vine's Complete Expository Dictionary of the Old and New Testament Words*, (Nashville, TN : Thomas Nelson, Inc., 1996), 18.
43. J. D. Douglas and Merrill C. Tenney, *New International Bible Dictionary*, (Grand Rapids, MI : The Zondervan Corporation, 1987), 230.
44. Ibid., 897.
45. Ibid., 897.

When you buy a book from **AMG Publishers**, **Living Ink Books**, or **God and Country Press**, you are helping to make disciples of Jesus Christ around the world.

How? AMG Publishers and its imprints are ministries of **AMG (*Advancing the Ministries of the Gospel*) International**, a non-denominational evangelical Christian mission organization ministering in over 30 countries around the world. Profits from the sale of AMG Publishers books are poured into the outreaches of AMG International.

AMG International Mission Statement

AMG exists to advance with compassion the command of Christ to evangelize and make disciples around the world through national workers and in partnership with like-minded Christians.

AMG International Vision Statement

We envision a day when everyone on earth will have at least one opportunity to hear and respond to a clear presentation of the Gospel of Jesus Christ and have the opportunity to grow as a disciple of Christ.

To learn more about AMG International and how you can pray for or financially support this ministry, please visit
www.amginternational.org.